BUILDING SELF-ESTEEM AND CONFIDENCE IN YOURSELF AND YOUR CHILD

BUILDING SELF-ESTEEM AND CONFIDENCE IN YOURSELF AND YOUR CHILD

C.E. Rollins and Jan Dargatz

Galahad Books   New York

Published in 1994 by

Galahad Books
A division of Budget Book Service, Inc.
386 Park Avenue South
New York, NY 10016

Galahad Books is a registered trademark of Budget Book Service, Inc.

Published by arrangement with Thomas Nelson Inc., Publishers.

Library of Congress Catalog Card Number: 93-80404

ISBN: 0-88365-857-7

Printed in the United States of America.

Contents

I. Build Your Self-Esteem and Confidence

To
Fred and Jan
and
Les and Bobi
with thanksgiving for
your lives and love

★ Contents

★ Introduction

We aren't born with high self-esteem and confidence. We must acquire them. From someone, somewhere.

The ideal purveyors of self-esteem and confidence are our parents. They sometimes fail, however. Generally, their failure is through unintentional neglect, oversight, or rejection created in part by circumstances over which they have little or no control. They rarely intend to fail at providing us a good foundation of self-value or the life skills we need to face adulthood with confidence. In many cases, *their* parents failed to provide for them all that they needed, and they simply are passing along a lack of good parenting skills. Unfortunately, we are capable of understanding that far better as adults than as children.

As children we only feel intuitively that our parents aren't giving us all that we need and that we are falling short of their full approval. We don't know that areas of the inner spirit are being dwarfed or untapped. We only know that we have an ache for something more. Hurts take root. Inner wounds fester. And we emerge as adults who are still hurt and wounded, now knowing a little more clearly our deficiencies and sensing a little more acutely our incompleteness, shortcomings, and inadequacies.

What can we do? First, we must forgive our parents. Failing to forgive them only keeps us riding the emotional merry-go-rounds of the past. Forgiveness frees us from their influence and allows us to face adulthood squarely.

Second, we must face our hurts and our inadequacies—defining them the best we can and determining the best ways in which we can heal ourselves or put ourselves into a position where others can assist us in the healing process.

Third, we must make a conscious decision to move toward wholeness. We must decide within ourselves that we *will* become whole adults. The decision to build self-esteem and confidence is ultimately a definitive move toward becoming a more complete person, whole in spirit, mind, emotions, body, and relationships.

Some individuals are the products of bona fide child abuse—physical, sexual, emotional, spiritual. In these cases the pain inflicted is intentional, or at least conscious, on the part of the perpetrator and far more damaging to the victim. Forgiveness may be harder to grant. The wounds may take longer to heal. But the process of healing *is* possible. Nobody, no matter how difficult the early years, needs to remain shackled forever by a deficient self-concept or a lack of personal confidence.

Finally, a vast number of persons experienced wonderful childhoods only to suffer abuse as adults from other adults—perhaps spouses, supervisors, teachers, or even "friends." The abuse may come in the form of rejection. In these cases of adult-onset abuse, the person's otherwise healthy self-esteem and confidence suffer a severe whack, generally from the blind side. What was once believed with full assurance is suddenly shaken; what was once taken for granted is suddenly found to be shifting; what was once regarded as truth is suddenly suspect; what was once counted on is suddenly questioned.

Again, the process of growth is essentially the same: forgiving the hurtful party, facing one's wounds, and making a determined effort to become whole again.

This section is divided into two parts:

(1) a set of "foundational choices" that are basic to becoming whole or to regaining wholeness;

(2) a set of "practical action steps"—things to do to fill in the gaps of one's life, to repair the breaches, to heal the wounds.

Achieving healthy self-regard and confidence to face not only the "future" but the challenges of the next twenty-four hours is not easy. It is doable. It is always a highly personal challenge. I hope this book helps you along the way.

Foundational
Choices

1 ★ Choose Truth

Many of us would like to live forever in fantasy-lands of our own creation—sweeping evidence of reality under every magic carpet we can find. The concept we develop of ourselves in fantasyland, however, is inevitably *not* a true one.

To gain or regain a healthy self-identity, you must first choose to face the truth about yourself and then decide what to do about it.

Ask yourself these two key questions:

1. Can I recognize a lie when I hear one? Very often we aren't aware, or refuse to face the fact, that what we are being told simply isn't true—about events, about relationships and, most important, about ourselves. Often, we let proclamations of "love" cloud the truth. *"He said he loved me, so I believed that what he told me about myself was true." "She lied to me all the time, but it was too painful to face the fact that someone who loved me would lie to me."*

2. *Do I tune out the truth or deny it?* If
the answer is yes, ask yourself why. Why would
you choose a lie over truth? Do you perceive truth
as more painful than lies? In the long run, the lie
always brings the greater pain. When you face the
truth squarely with an optimistic attitude that "if
it's wrong I can fix it, if it's sin I can repent of it, if
it's bad I can seek a way to get to good," the truth
is not only liberating but the first step toward a
better tomorrow.

Several other questions related to truth are important to consider:

- Who is telling me who I am, what I can do,
  and defining my status and worth in life?

To whom are you giving the power for your definition? Is it a mother who died twenty years ago? A
spouse? An adult child? You are the product of a
series of definitions about yourself that you have
accepted as being true. It helps to go back periodically and reevaluate to whom you have given this
"power of definition."

- Are the people from whom I am deriving definitions of myself trustworthy?

What is their motivation for telling you things
about yourself? What do they get out of it? Could
they be wrong? Could they be misinformed? Could

they be lying purposefully? Could they be inadvertently tearing you down to build themselves up? Could they be projecting on you their own feelings of inadequacy?

- Is the information I am taking into my being and adopting as true actually rooted in reality?

Can you cite evidence that supports the conclusions being drawn about yourself? Are you taking things at face value without substantiating them? Are you cross-examining the witnesses to your life?

In seeking the truth, choose to associate with those who tell the truth. Ask why persons believe what they say about you. Ask upon what evidence they base their conclusions. Question their motives.

And above all . . . if the "truth" they proclaim about you is all bad, demand that they also tell you the "truth" about you that is good. Only then can you even begin to achieve a balanced report. Be highly suspicious of the people who point out only your flaws and failures and never applaud your strengths and successes. They aren't telling you the whole story. And a partial story isn't truth.

2 ★ Choose Joy

Joy is a choice. Most people don't think so, but it is. We can choose to rejoice in life, or we can choose to be morose.

Sadness is a valid emotion. Sorrow is a part of the human experience. The continuum of emotions available to all of us includes the negative. There's a dark side to each one of us. In choosing joy, we are not negating the existence or the value of pain. We are simply choosing not to dwell there emotionally.

More Than Happiness Joy is more than happiness. Happiness is contingent on outer circumstances—the arrival of a happy surprise, the dawn of a bright morning, the cozy fireplace feeling of being curled up in the warmth of family love. Joy is rooted not in the external but in the internal. It's an attitude based on these beliefs:

- Life is important.
- Life has direction.
- Life has meaning and purpose.

- Life holds potential.
- Direction, meaning, and potential are all worth seeking and achieving.

Joy is rooted in the belief that life is *good* and that you are *good* and that both have the capacity for being better.

More Than Positive Thinking   Joy is more than positive thinking. It's more than getting up and saying repeatedly to the mirror, "I'm the greatest." Joy isn't "worked up"; it's brought forth. Joy is the spark at the core of your being that you *refuse* to allow to be extinguished, no matter how fierce the winds of woe are blowing or how dark the circumstances.

How can you increase your joy level today? Joy comes when you stare down fear and say, "I will not let fear swamp my boat. I will not let darkness overtake me. I will not let failure consume me. I will praise God and exult in life—no matter what."

Choose joy today. Choose to perceive yourself as a joyful person. You have the power to be that— no matter what other difficulties may lie ahead in your growth toward confidence and high self-esteem.

3 ★ Choose to Live

The person who has experienced a severe loss nearly always goes through at least one period in which he wishes he could crawl in a hole somewhere and pull it in over his head. Sometimes the wish becomes a strong desire to escape, withdraw, or just plain disappear for a while.

The emotional wounds that come with a loss are very real and very painful. We should never discount their impact or their potential to fester and turn into a malignant bitterness over time. The reaction of desiring to flee when wounded is a normal one. When the self has been injured in any way, the desire to withdraw from life is to be expected.

The critical moment comes, however, when you must choose to live again. Choose to reemerge. Choose to reembrace life. Choose to go on!

Choose a Rich, Full, Wonderful Life

Don't simply choose to survive. Try to look beyond the pain of the moment and envision a life in which you are *not* hanging on by your fingernails or just scraping by. Envision a future day in which you are once again strong, prosperous, and emotionally vibrant.

Choose a Life That Has Meaning and Purpose

Establish a reason in your own heart and mind to go forward in life. You may need to talk to a professional counselor in helping to determine what *you* still see as a "purpose" or use for your life.

Each person has something to give. Including *you!* What can you still contribute to others? Think about it. Write it down. Then . . . choose to give it. In so doing, you'll be choosing to live and not die.

4 ★ Choose Today

Every morning offers you a new opportunity to start over—to enjoy a success, to be all that you can be, to live life to the fullest.

The tendency when faced with a severe blow to esteem or confidence is to dwell on what once was.

Closing the Door on the Past The person who is down on himself nearly always blames himself for the failures of the past. It's helpful to sort out the past in order to

- determine what part of the failure was truly yours.
- analyze what you did that contributed to the failure—the decisions you made, the actions you took, the timing of your actions, the faulty rationale or incorrect evidence upon which you acted, and so forth.
- resolve what it is that you should have done, which, in effect, is a resolution about what you would do if faced with a similar set of circumstances in the future.

Forgive yourself for your part of the failure, make whatever amends and recompenses you can make or you believe should be made, and then close the door on the past. Choose *not* to dwell there. Choose not to live your life looking in the rearview mirror.

Keeping the Future at Arm's Length A second tendency of the person with low self-esteem is to look at the future and say, "I don't have what it takes to be successful again (or ever)." The key question to ask yourself is this: Why not? What has changed about *you*—not what has changed about the circumstances around you? You may have been deeply wounded, rejected, or abused, but the core of the inner you—your talents, personality traits, experiences, acquired skills, inherent creativity—can never be stolen or destroyed by another person. That part of you can only be sealed over by you. You do *have* what it takes to forge a wonderful future.

- Learn to live a *successful* day. Include in your daily plan the acquisition of one or two daily habits that you consider to be good.

Set one or two goals of "things to do" for yourself personally. Focus on a goal or two for the workday. Take stock as the day closes and contemplate for a few moments what you did right during the day.

- If you find that you are not successful in reaching your daily goals, readjust them so that you will be!

You may be biting off more than you can chew. Your successful day may include nothing more than the fact that you got dressed, ate three meals, walked the dog, took out the trash, made two phone calls, and went to the grocery store. Success is what *you* define it to be.

What happens when you string together a series of mostly successful days? You end up with a successful life. Choose to live today. It's the only time you truly can control.

5 ★ Choose to Grow

Do you remember how you felt as a child in the presence of grown-ups? Grown-ups had it easy. They could do what they wanted when they wanted, and they could call the shots.

But if anything, life seems to get harder with time. Adults certainly don't get to call all the shots they'd like to call. You come to realize, however, that it's good always to be growing.

Growing means changing. And change is scary. It requires a risk. Choose to take it. Every person I've ever known who undertook a growth change said as he or she emerged on the other side, "I'm glad I did that. It was worth it. I'm better off today than I was then."

Get Professional Counsel You may find great opportunities for growth by talking with an expert in the area in which you desire to grow. If you need career advice, talk to a career counselor. If you need psychological help, talk to a psychologist. If you need spiritual help, seek out a minister or priest who is trained in counseling.

Gain New Information To keep growing mentally, you need a steady dose of "input." Information comes in a wide variety of packages: courses, manuals, magazines, movies, galleries, museums, libraries. Avail yourself of the best teachers you can find.

Gather New Experiences Ever been on a roller coaster? Ever seen the ocean? Ever climbed a mountain?

A part of the growing process in a relationship—personal or professional—invariably seems to require confrontation. Learn to fight fairly with those around you. Learn ways in which to explore and communicate and set goals. Getting past the confrontation may involve a mutual decision to pursue counseling, gain information, or gather experience . . . together.

There's really no such thing as "just maintaining forever." Maintaining is possible for a while, and the person who suffers a blow to his self-esteem sometimes needs to "just maintain." (Often, that's all he can do. In those cases, maintaining a regimen of sleeping, eating, working, playing is actually growth—it's building up strength.) Eventually, we all need to move beyond what seems to be a "just maintaining" state. In the long run of life, what isn't growing is starting to die.

Choose growth. It's a part of choosing life.

6 ★ Choose to Forgive

"Forgive and forget" is a phrase known to all of us. It's bad advice, however, because it's not possible for any of us ever to forgive and forget.

Forgiveness is possible. Forgetting isn't.

No matter how hard you may try, you can never truly forget an experience you've had. Brain researchers tell us that any person with a normal brain can be made to recall *any* incident that has occurred in his or her life. You do not carry all of the information you have in your conscious mind, but you never lose any information once you have acquired it. It's always lurking within someplace.

The good news is that forgiveness brings a sense of order, resolution, and meaning to all of the events of our past that we cannot forget. In that, forgiveness heals.

Not the Prosecutor It takes tremendous emotional and mental energy to be another person's prosecutor. You constantly must appraise what she did in the light of current consequences. You must think about her continually to try to understand her motives for the crime. You must always be looking for evidence related to her behavior. Actually, it's emotionally exhausting to stand as prosecutor for another person.

Not the Judge   It also takes wisdom that none of us has to be another person's judge. You can never fully understand another person—know all of his reasons for doing and saying certain things, know everything about his background or personality, or know with certainty that your "sentence" for him is the most just or redemptive one.

The forgiving person says,

- "I think you were a lousy parent. But I no longer hold that against you. I take the responsibility for my adulthood on myself. I forgive you for what you did, and I release you from having an ongoing influence in my life today."
- "I think you were an abusive spouse. But I no longer want to dwell on your abuse. I mentally and emotionally am letting you go so that I can be free."
- "I think you were wrong to fire me. But I refuse to focus my thoughts on you any longer. I release you from my mind and my heart. I choose instead to look forward to my next job."
- "I don't believe you really tried to help me or

to assist my growth. But I choose to forgive you for not being all that I think you should have been for me. I choose to be responsible for my own life, to get the assistance I need, and to make the growth I desire."

Forgiveness frees you to deal with your present and make plans for your future. It puts you into a position where you are no longer "under the influence" of another person's critical behavior—including the behavior that damages your self-esteem and injures your confidence.

7 ★ Choose to Receive

You didn't acquire unhealthy self-esteem on your own. Somebody helped you along in the process of your thinking poorly about yourself. Through critical comments, negative put-downs, or lack of attention or positive feedback, the person (or persons) assisted in your lack of self-development.

The converse is also true. You won't acquire healthy self-esteem entirely on your own.

Choose to be around people who have healthy self-esteem Talk to them and watch them. Learn from them. Ask their advice.

Choose to be around people who will build you up Everybody needs a cheerleader. That doesn't mean the other person is blind to your faults or impervious to your bad behavior—only that the person *wants* to see you succeed and grow and is willing to cheer you on.

Choose to associate with people who are growing Their enthusiasm for life will inspire you. The insights they draw from their own growth will help you.

Choose to align yourself with people who truly want to be your friend and whom you want to befriend in return There are millions of positive, encouraging, growing people in the world. You can't have all of them as friends. Seek to develop a few close friendships in which you are both generous giver and generous receiver.

Choose to associate with people who have a giving attitude toward the world Associate with people who want to make a contribution to life, who want to see problems solved, needs met, improvements made, bad situations resolved. Don't expect to be the object of their giving as much as a cogiver with them.

Choose to receive the good things that people desire to give you Don't shun their constructive help. Don't disregard their compliments. Don't turn them away when they offer to be with you in a difficult moment. Open up and receive what they have for you.

The person with low self-esteem is often wary. Too many people have hurt her in the guise of trying to help. He has been wounded in the name of love. If that's the case in your life, you'll need to make a conscious choice to open up and receive.

- Choose your givers wisely.
- Choose to receive only what helps you.
- Choose to receive only what you can contain.

The more good, positive, upbuilding information and opinions you receive into yourself about yourself, the more your self-esteem will grow.

Practical Action
Steps

8 ★ Just Say No

Is someone telling you . . .
"You're not good enough,"
"You aren't acceptable,"
"You don't have what it takes,"
"You're unlovable,"
"You're not worth it"?
Just say, "No. You're wrong about me."

Stand your ground! Don't lie down and let another person trample over your soul.

Before you adopt a strong defensive position, make certain you understand fully the statement being made about you. With as much control and quiet resolve as you can muster, question the person until you get to the real intent of the statement:

- "Are you saying that I don't have what it takes because I lack certain skills or training, or is it because you think I'm defective as a person?"
- "Are you saying that I'm unlovable because you lack the capacity to love me, or are there certain attributes or behaviors that you don't

like?" (Always assume that like and love are two different emotions, and that they don't always accompany each other.)

- "On what evidence are you concluding that I'm unacceptable? Is it my qualifications or my personhood that makes me unacceptable?"

It's Your Right   It's your right to have an answer to accusations against your personhood. The answers may not be what you want to hear, but listen very closely to them to learn all that you need to learn. If, indeed, you lack specific skills and attributes, take the position that those are things you can learn or develop. The reason you are being rejected has to do with qualifications, not the quality of your personhood.

If, on the other hand, the statement is against who you are—calling into question your right to exist, your basic human rights, or your legal rights—stand firm and challenge the remark. Say, "I disagree with you. I think you have an erroneous (or limited) perception of me." State your reasons for drawing that conclusion.

"But what if the person is bigger than I am?" you may ask. (Which may also be stated as "stronger than I am," "more powerful than I am," or "smarter than I am.") Stand your ground anyway.

You Deserve Better Even if someone attempts to use force against you, declare, "You have no right to do this to me or to say this to me. I deserve better."

You may need to appeal to a higher authority if you feel you are being accused unjustly.

You may need to seek legal action.

You may need to get away. (There's little point in standing your ground to the point of being murdered or maimed.)

In so doing, however, make sure you are taking an action that you choose. Even if you shout it to the wind . . . or whisper it to your mirror . . . make a proclamation within yourself, "I am valuable. I am worthy to be loved. I may make mistakes, but I am a person of worth."

Say no to the person who attempts to put you down or chip away at your self-worth. Say no to the person who attempts to undermine your self-confidence. In so doing, you are saying yes to yourself.

9 ★ Don't Belittle Yourself

You've probably heard someone say,
   "Oh, I don't deserve this."
   Or "I'm just a nobody."
   Or "That's out of my league."
   Are you guilty of making statements like that about yourself?
   Are you guilty of calling yourself stupid or any other of a vast number of derogatory terms?
   If so . . . stop it.

Never, Never, Never Belittle Yourself
We each have enough trouble withstanding the jealous, unwise, careless, hurtful remarks of others. We don't need to heap even more coals on our own heads.
   What happens when you make a negative remark about yourself?

- First, you reinforce that very idea in your own mind.

Your own two ears are usually the closest ears to your own mouth. If you believe yourself, you begin to think of yourself as you describe yourself!

- Second, you plant the idea in the minds of others.

Soon, they'll be saying to themselves, "Well, if she thinks she's stupid, she probably is," or "If he thinks he's a fool, chances are that he knows what he's talking about." Others begin to think of you exactly as you ask them to think of you, and the next thing you know, they'll be treating you according to the way you've suggested they treat you —as if you're a fool, a klutz, or a loser!

If you claim to another person that you don't deserve something . . . next time you probably won't receive it. If you tell another person that you're worthless . . . the next time you come up for a raise, you probably won't get it. If you claim to be a nobody . . . next time you probably won't be invited to go along.

Play It Straight "But," you may protest, "I'm just teasing."

Don't do it. When it comes to who you are, play it straight.

"But," you say, "if I don't say something like that, people will think I'm proud."

You don't need to say something prideful. Rather

than say something derogatory about yourself, don't say anything at all! Or just say, "Thank you" or "Wow" or "What a country!" or "I have it on the highest authority that I'll do better next time!"

You can be surprised that you won the award, but don't say, "Oh, you should have chosen someone else."

You can be thankful that you received the honor, but don't say, "Wow, I really don't deserve this."

You can be intrigued by why someone asked you to come along or be a part or take the new role, but don't say, "Are you sure you chose the right person?"

People tend to think of you as you tell them to think. Therefore, tell them well.

10 ★ Stare Down Your Greatest Fear

Fear is the silent companion of low self-esteem. People who struggle with low self-esteem usually express a deep feeling of fear. In many cases, that feeling of fear is referred to as a rather "uneasy feeling," a "worry," or a feeling of being "troubled." When questioned about it, the person often doesn't know what is bothering him, or he may be able to describe uneasy situations without being able to label the fear.

The fear is ultimately one common to all of us: the fear of being alone. Scientists have told us for decades that all babies are born with two fears: the fear of falling, and the fear of sudden noises. Both fears are closely associated with birth: the quiet, muffled noises of the womb are suddenly disrupted as the baby "falls" from its mother's womb into a completely new and much noisier environment. What a traumatic experience that would be for us adults if we found ourselves in a similar situation, even if we knew the outcome would be tolerable!

Separation is also a part of the birthing process.

With the cutting of the umbilical cord we are no longer vitally connected to another human being in what had seemed to us to be an inseparable relationship. In many ways, we all long for that closeness, intimacy, and feeling of being "one" with another throughout our lives. The fear of losing connection seems to be a basic fear rooted in the emotions, just as fears of falling and loud noises are rooted in physical instincts.

Are you fearful today? Do you feel as if something is bothering you deep down inside your spirit?

Face that fear. Name it. Confront it.

Admit It to Yourself "I'm afraid of being alone. I don't want to be alone. I don't like the idea of being alone."

Face Up to the Fact "I am alone. I've been alone for years, and I've survived. Even though I may have wonderful relationships with others, I will ultimately be alone. Even in the best marriage, the most loving family environment, the most meaningful work relationship . . . I am an individual who is responsible for my own actions, ideas, choices, and responsibilities. That's life. And I can make the most of it."

Recognize It "Every other person on the planet is also afraid of being alone. Nobody wants to be alone any more than I do. If I am rejected or disconnected from one person, there are literally hundreds of thousands of other people with whom I might establish a connection."

Be Hopeful "Since we are all longing for a connection, I will do my best to reach out to others who are just as fearful of being alone as I am. I will not expect them to do more for me than they can do; I will do all I can do to be a loyal friend (spouse, family member, colleague) to them."

Fear cripples us from being ourselves and from exercising our talents and pursuing our potential.

When, out of fear, you don't express yourself freely, you cut off a part of who you are and what you can be. You limit yourself. Low self-esteem and lack of confidence result because ultimately, in limiting your actions, you convince yourself that you can't do certain things or aren't capable of reaching certain goals.

Self-esteem begins to grow when you face your greatest fear and stare it down.

11 ★ Conduct a Personal Inventory

The person with low self-esteem rarely sees beyond her own nose. She is often far more preoccupied with herself than the person with high self-esteem. Growth occurs when a person is able to stand back and take an objective look at herself—to appraise herself as she would someone else.

If you have trouble doing this, ask someone to help you be objective about yourself. Choose someone you trust to tell you the truth—a trusted friend, a minister, or a professional counselor.

Put Your Inventory on Paper That way, you'll be able to refer to it later and be encouraged at seeing your growth over time. No personal inventory is ever final. It should constantly be in a state of positive change.

List Your Assets Fixed personal assets are those with which you were born—such as a strong physical constitution, family members you consider good role models, or musical ability. Note all of your personality strengths and talents. Liquid assets are those things you have acquired in life—training, education, experiences, associations, and friendships. (Sometimes friends and colleagues are the finest assets you have!)

Identify Your Goals

Your goals and dreams are a part of who you are as a person. They are often the reason you act as you do. Generally speaking, the person with low self-esteem has lower and fewer goals than the person with high self-esteem. If you don't have any goals, take this opportunity to set some!

Identify Your Beliefs

What do you feel strongly about? What are your spiritual values? What is your ethical code? Your value system is the "energy" behind your actions; it nearly always correlates with the intensity of your motivation. Very often, the person with low self-esteem loses sight of her beliefs, or her value system becomes weak. Writing down what you believe provides a good exercise in reappraising your inner spiritual life.

Identify Your Liabilities

Take a moment to question what you listed as your liabilities. Ask yourself why you placed them in that category. You may be relating your liabilities to your goals—using them as excuses for why you can't succeed or aren't succeeding. That's rarely valid.

All of your "liabilities" are liquid. The more closely you look at them, the more likely you are to erase them from the list. Make that the final part of your personal inventory.

Identify Specific Actions to Turn Liabilities into Assets   What can you do by yourself? What requires assistance from others? Where can you get that assistance? Set a timetable for yourself to convert liabilities into assets. Some perceived liabilities may never become true "assets" to you, but they can at least become neutralized so that they really don't stand in the way of your achieving your goals or acting on your beliefs.

Now, stand back and take a look at the overall picture. If you are truly objective, you'll probably find that you have a great many more assets— counting your dreams, beliefs, goals, and friends as assets—than you have liabilities. Your liabilities generally can be converted to assets or at least become neutral factors in your life.

Take stock of who you *really* are!

12 ★ Map Out a Plan

After you have completed your personal inventory, take a second related step and map out a personal growth plan.

Review Your Assets What can you do to strengthen them? How can you enrich your friendships and professional associations? What can you do to gain more information or acquire more skills in your area of interest or expertise?

Review Your Goals Are they realistic? Are they really ones you want to *work* to achieve? Eliminate the goals that are just wishful thinking or idle daydreaming. Eliminate all goals based on random chance. (Winning the state lottery is *not* an acceptable goal—it's a fanciful wish!) Break your goals into subgoals or components. Identify a series of small steps you can take to get to your final destination.

How do some of your goals interrelate? Are there any areas in which you may be able to reach two goals with one activity?

Review Your Beliefs How can you act on
them? What specific things can you do to test, reinforce, or activate the things you hold as important
values?

Doing and Being Make lists. Set timetables.
Focus on a regimen that will help you make your
days, weeks, and months count toward the accomplishment of the goals important to you.

"All this doing," you may moan. "When do I get
to the being—the relaxing moments, the taking of
life as it comes?"

Lists don't preclude spontaneity. In many cases,
they allow for it! Schedules don't preclude quiet
times, recreation, or periods of "soaking" in beauty
and rest. They can accommodate downtime.

For most people, doing and being are so tightly
interrelated they really can't be separated. We are
what we do; we act based on who we are. Even the
most peaceful, laid-back person *does* certain things
that create that feeling within his being.

The real issue is one of intentionality. Do you
want to have healthier self-esteem? Then you probably need to focus your life more. Do you want
more confidence? Then there's a necessary doing
of certain things to achieve it.

13 ★ Stop Comparing

The person with low self-esteem and confidence nearly always has developed the bad habit of comparing himself or herself to others.

- "I'm just not as pretty as Susie."
- "I'm not as smart as Gerald."
- "I didn't come from the same privileged background as Margaret."
- "I didn't have the same opportunity for education as Barrett."

Stop comparing. You're engaging in a lie.

A lie? Yes! Comparisons are usually based on inaccurate information and are thus false to some degree.

In the First Place You don't know all there is to know about that other person. You don't really know Gerald's IQ or his aptitude scores in various areas of learning. You don't really know all the details of Margaret's background or the inside story on the financial aid package that made Barrett's education possible. Every person has something to overcome to achieve success in life. Every "win" has its price in terms of time, effort, and resources.

In the Second Place   Comparisons are often used as excuses for failure: *"I didn't get the job (or the promotion, the raise, the date, the award, the honor) . . . because . . . I'm not as smart as Gerald (as pretty as Susie, and so forth)."* Again, that's probably not the case.

By using an excuse, you are lying to yourself. You aren't facing up to the real reasons behind what you perceive to be a loss. You aren't acknowledging the fact that you were popping gum during the interview, your appearance was sloppy, you used bad grammar (which you need to relearn), you didn't fill out the application completely, you ridiculed the other person, you don't have the proper qualifications, or any of an infinite number of other reasons.

In gaining self-esteem and confidence, you must first tell the truth about yourself and limit your concern to yourself. You must take the blame for your failures to be able to applaud your successes.

14 ★ Stand Tall

This observation holds true regardless of age, sex, race, physical stature, or beauty:

> *The person with high self-esteem stands up straight, sits tall, and walks with boldness. The person with low self-esteem slouches, slinks, bows his head down, curls his shoulders forward, and frequently sits in knots.*

No matter how much makeup the person may have on, the precision of the hairstyle, the gleam on the boots, or the cost of the clothing . . . regardless of any of the jewelry or related accessories (including the model of car) . . . a person who stands tall, sits tall, and walks tall considers herself to be a woman of value and inner strength, a woman with the potential for success.

The minute you make the decision within yourself to grow in self-esteem and confidence, make a second decision: I'm going to "move tall" this day forward.

Shoulders back and head up.

A bold stride—even if you are just walking from one room to the next in your own home.

A square-to-the-world attitude!

Physical Well-Being   When you take on a new posture, you'll feel better physically. Good posture is linked in many ways to overall health.

Psychological Well-Being   You'll feel better psychologically. Not all signals in your being come from the brain first; in the case of posture, your body is also sending a signal to your brain. If you walk tall, you'll soon be thinking tall. Reach for the sky with your head, and you tend to reach for the sky with your attitude.

When you communicate a message of strength, authority, and self-value, others will treat you with more respect. You'll find that others are less likely to try to put you down. The more they treat you with respect, the more likely you are to feel positive about who you are.

Think "tall and straight" today!

15 ★ Smile

Nothing warms the heart, including your own heart, like a smile! Researchers are discovering more and more about the helpful chemicals released into the bloodstream as the result of laughter, smiles, and positive attitudes. The "merry heart" described by sages of old really "does good, like medicine."

Apart from the physical benefits of a smiling attitude lie the emotional ones. A person simply cannot laugh uproariously for a prolonged period without feeling a little bit better on the inside, too.

Smile at Yourself Learn to laugh at your foibles. The human condition is laughable in many ways; we all act the fool and perform the ridiculous at times—even the person who seems most poised and coolheaded. Don't laugh at yourself with ridicule; laugh at the fact that sometimes you do yourself in, generally in the craziest ways at the least opportune times. Turn loose and laugh *with* yourself, not *at* yourself.

Smile to Yourself Greet yourself in the morning with a grin. More important, call up memories that bring a smile to your face. That's one of the wonderful benefits of pleasurable experiences —you can recall them later for a second, even hundredth, moment of enjoyment.

Smile at Others Strangers. Friends. Co-workers. Your own family members. Spread the joy around. It's difficult to maintain a frown for very long in the presence of someone who is smiling!

Get back in touch with those things that once caused you to laugh with a hold-your-sides, belly-shaking laugh. Let go and have a little fun.

The person with low self-esteem tends to take life—and herself, or lack of self—far too seriously. Lighten up.

16 ★ Get Up and Get Out

The person with low self-esteem often hides from the world.

Set for yourself a minimal goal of achieving the "three *G*'s" every day.

Get Up Get out of bed. Don't stay there. If you return to bed during the day for a nap, don't get back into your nightwear—lie down with your street clothes on.

By getting out of bed, you are exerting an attitude of "I choose to be well."

Of course, you can sleep in occasionally, you can retire early, or you can choose to spend an entire vacation day lounging around in your robe and pajamas. But as the norm of your life, choose to be out of bed, not in it.

Get Dressed Shower (or bathe). Shave (if you do). Comb your hair. Get dressed. Put on your makeup (if you wear it). Face the day. You may not leave the neighborhood, but look as if you are ready to face the public.

Getting dressed helps you adopt the attitude that you are ready to do something or experience something—that you are expecting something to happen in your life and you're ready for it!

Get Out of the House   Even if you just walk around the block or sit outside on the porch, deck, or patio, get out of the four walls of your own space and give yourself the opportunity to interact with nature and with people. Both are God's gifts to you. Learn to see them as such and to avail yourself of the good things they have to offer you.

In all of your "getting" self-esteem . . . get up and get going!

17 ★ Have a Little Pep Talk with Yourself

Sometimes it helps to be your own cheerleader.

Give Voice to Your Good Opinions about Yourself Don't just "think" good about yourself; speak those good words aloud. You'll hear yourself, and the words will have a double opportunity to take root in your spirit. Say to yourself,

- "I can do this."
- "I'm worth it."
- "I'm able to learn this."
- "I'm going to try this."

People with low self-esteem get that way in part because they don't have someone else telling them how valuable and worthy they are. If you don't have someone else around to tell you how great you are, to applaud your bright moments, or to reinforce your good qualities—or if you missed out on having someone build you up in the past—tell yourself!

Readjust Your Memories   Go back in memory to times when you succeeded, performed well, or did a good job—especially those times when nobody seemed to notice or say anything to you—and compliment yourself. Say aloud, "You know, you really did a good job in making that model airplane," or "You sang every word of the song while lots of children around you were lip-synching," or "That was a great water color painting you did," or "I'm proud of you for getting a 90 on your history test."

Take a clue from the tennis courts. Players pump themselves up during a match. It works for them, and it will work for you!

18 ★ Adopt Healthy Habits

The person with low self-esteem frequently falls into a habit of not caring for herself. That often includes physical care as well as emotional care.

Adopt a healthy daily regimen.

Good Nutrition Fuel yourself with the freshest foods and the purest water. Avoid "junk" foods and foods high in salt, fat, and sugar.

Regular Meals Three squares a day and an optional snack—that's the routine followed by most health care facilities in the nation and the finest spas around the world! If it's good for them, it's a good policy for your home.

If you have difficulty cooking or you simply don't want to cook, you still have lots of options. Order in. Eat out. Hire a cook. These options may sound expensive, but many times they are less expensive than purchasing food that you end up throwing away.

Sufficient Sleep   Eight or nine quality hours of sleep, uninterrupted, are considered the goal for most people (as supported by recent research). You may need to adopt an earlier lights-out policy at your house; you may need to adjust your schedule; you may need to quit working into the wee hours of the morning; you may need to make sleep a priority. Whatever it takes, get your *Z*'s.

People Contact   For at least a portion of your day, be with other people with whom you can spend relaxed moments and have unhurried conversation—to talk over the hurdles overcome or faced, your successes, the latest joke you heard, the funny thing that happened on the way home, the new products you saw in the store, the up-to-date news in the world, your community, your neighborhood, your life, your opinions.

Play Time   Devote at least one part of each day to fun. If exercise is "work" to you, it doesn't count. Your fun activity may be a hobby, a game, a sport, a fix-it project, a movie, or a book. Do something that completely takes your mind off work and problems. If you work with your hands all day, your fun activity may be something that engages your mind. If you work with your mind all day, try doing something with your hands. TV doesn't count as play. While it may entertain, it doesn't replenish. Choose an activity about which you can say afterward, "That sure was fun. I had a great time." Indulge in laughter.

Centering Time Set aside at least a few minutes of each day for quiet solitude. Learn to enjoy being alone. Use the time for reading inspirational literature . . . for praying . . . for just thinking. Focus on the larger issues of life, not personal problems. Daydream. Imagine. Think big thoughts.

A daily discipline with these components sends a signal to your psyche: you have balance; you have health. The healthy balanced person is a prime candidate for high self-esteem!

19 ★ Say No to Chemical Snares

Even as you say yes to health on a daily basis, say no to those things that would rob you of your health.

The person with low self-esteem sometimes turns to chemicals—including alcohol—as a means of bolstering confidence or improving self-perception.

In the long run, chemicals don't improve confidence or self-esteem; they help only to mask—temporarily—the lack of esteem and confidence.

Say no to chemicals you don't need for normal bodily function Assume that any chemicals you take are ones required by your particular body for restoring normal function. For example, an aspirin may help you get rid of a headache. Don't assume that you need two aspirin every four hours for the rest of your life to keep a headache from returning. On the other hand, if you are a diabetic who is insulin dependent, take that insulin. Your particular body needs it for normal function.

Don't assume that any medication you take is going to be necessary for a lifetime   Some medications may be in this category, especially those for chronic heart patients. Other medications should be allowed to run their course, with no expectation of your refilling a prescription. Don't assume that because you are prescribed a tranquilizer or an antidepressant to get through a particularly difficult period you will always need the medication. Most drugs are prescribed for singular ailments that pass within a month!

Take prescription medicines only as they are prescribed   Don't take more than one prescribed medication at a time without checking first with your physician. Always ask about side effects, especially those that might occur when two or more medications react with each other inside your body. Never assume that if one pill works well, two pills will work twice as well.

Never take a chemical to enhance your ability to do something   Whether you want to relax, have more energy, be more creative, work longer hours, or improve muscle strength, such drugs will inevitably do you more harm than good.

Never take a chemical to enhance your perceived social status   Participating in "chemical events" enhances your status only with others who are participating—in other words, your status is enhanced only by those who are already addicted, misinformed, misled, rebellious, or unwise. Associating with those folks is detrimental to your self-esteem.

If you find that you are becoming addicted to a prescribed medication, talk to your doctor about safe ways to get off the drug   Don't attempt to go "cold turkey" or to detox yourself.

Face up to the fact that alcohol and nicotine are drugs   Don't get started on these substances. If you're already addicted, get help to free yourself. You'll feel better physically, and you'll have a great sense of victory in overcoming the addiction.

Chemically induced feelings of self-esteem are always a poor substitute for the real thing.

20 ★ Associate with High-Esteem People

Choose to be around people who are confident and have a balanced, healthy perspective about themselves. Choose to associate with individuals who value themselves and others. Choose to participate in activities and projects with men and women who are growing—who are setting high goals for themselves and are on the path toward achieving them.

You'll Be Inspired   You'll find that the hours spent in the presence of high-esteem people pass quickly and productively. You'll feel encouraged to try new things, and you'll gain a desire to do more and be more.

You'll Be Helped   People with high self-esteem are nearly always givers. They are frequently teachers or mentors at heart—people who desire to help others reach their full potential, even as they seek to reach their own. Accept their help and advice.

You'll Be Instructed   You'll learn by watching them—not only in the area of work skills but in the areas of communication and interpersonal skills. Be open to their suggestions.

Want to learn something? Find the person most confident in his knowledge of it or his ability in it!

In a famous art gallery one afternoon, a dozen or so art students were copying the great paintings before them. Their teacher said of this practice: "You must copy in order to learn technique, to get a foundation. Later, you can choose your own subjects and your own style." Good advice!

The more you associate with high-esteem people and the more you emulate their behaviors and mind-set, the more you'll esteem yourself, and the more others will regard you with greater respect.

21 ★ Treat Yourself

Indulge yourself occasionally. Just because.

- It might be taking a long relaxing bubble bath.
- It might be ordering a favorite food in a favorite restaurant.
- It might be exploring the shops in a certain area for an entire afternoon.
- It might be going to the movies all by yourself.

Whatever your choice of a treat, give yourself a dose of pleasure.

Inexpensive Indulgences You may need to hire a baby-sitter to indulge yourself. Do so! You need to feel good about yourself if you are ever going to transmit a good feeling to your child.

You need not, however, spend a great deal of money on your indulgence. The indulgence may be time alone. A walk in the park at noon may suffice, at no cost (and with the added benefit of exercise).

Occasional Indulgences   You shouldn't make a habit of your indulgence. Otherwise, it will soon cease to be a treat. A chocolate sundae every afternoon isn't an indulgence; it's overkill.

Choose an occasional indulgence that represents something you might not otherwise do or that you might expect someone else to do for you.

Buy yourself a bouquet of flowers. Enjoy them!

Give yourself an occasional gift.

About once a year, one fellow takes a roll of quarters and goes down to the local video arcade to play all of the games. "For two hours, I'm a carefree, spendthrift teenager again," he says. "The rest of the year I can be grown up."

You treat people you like. You gift people you respect or wish to honor. The acts are no less important when you are the recipient.

22 ★ Point Out the Positive

When someone calls attention to the negative about a situation or speaks a word of negative criticism, choose to speak up for the positive—especially if the negative comment is about you!

"I'm Me" What do you say when someone says to you, "You're not as good a cook as Sally," or "You're not as good an *anything* as someone else"? Respond, "Perhaps not. I agree with you that Sally is a good cook. But I'm probably a lot better than Sally at other things. I'm me. Sally's Sally. Each of us has different strengths and weaknesses. Let me remind you about one of my strengths."

"See My Good Points" What do you say when someone says to you, "You're a slob"? First, ask for a definition of the term. What is it that the person doesn't like? Insist on concrete statements. Don't deny the fact that you may be "part slob"; at the same time, don't take on a total identity of a slob! Respond, "There's some merit in what you say, and I'll work on it. But there's also a good side to me. Everybody has some good and bad points. I hope you can see my good points, too."

"What Do You Like?" What do you say when someone says to you, "I don't like the way you do your hair"? Respond, "Thank you for expressing your opinion. What do you like about me today?"

"I Have Strengths" Always bring a negative-commenting person back to the positive. Insist on being considered as a whole person with both bad and good qualities—flaws you are working on and strengths you are seeking to enhance.

At times, you may need to insist that the person admit the flaw is a small one, not one of cosmic proportions or importance. Few flaws are fatal, either to you or to others. You can respond, "Yes, I do have that fault. I'm working on it. I'm sorry it irritates you. But I also know that this isn't something of life-or-death consequences."

The person with low self-esteem frequently tunes in only to negative comments. He frequently fails to stand up for his own positive attributes. Insist that others speak positive things to you each time they speak negatives.

23 ★ Make Something with Your Hands

Create something with your own two hands. It might be something for utility or beauty or fun:

- Something you make out of wood—a piece of furniture, a frame, a doghouse, a birdfeeder, a deck, or a candlestick
- Something you paint or draw
- Something you sew by machine or hand
- Something you create in ceramic or clay—a piece of sculpture or something you spin out on a potter's wheel
- Something you put together—a model, a dollhouse for your little girl, or a swing set for the backyard

Achievement How does working with your hands relate to self-esteem? Projects made by hand have an obvious beginning, middle, and ending. When you're finished with the day's work, you can see your progress. When you're finished with the project, you can rejoice in your achievement. A finished handcraft says to you and to others, "I am a person capable of making things."

Skill   A project made by hand calls for skill. Your work may be crude because your skills aren't perfectly honed. That's OK. Consider it one of your "earlier works." The handmade object says to you and to others, "I have a skill. I'm still developing it, but the good news is that I'm growing in this ability. I'm capable of learning."

Planning   Made-by-hand projects require some planning and nearly always an ability to read and follow instructions. The finished product says, "I can think, and I can translate what I read into something I can do. I am an intelligent person!"

The handmade object is a reflection of you—your intelligence, your artistry and craftsmanship, your ability to make choices in life, your time and, above all, your ability to set a goal and discipline yourself to reach it, piece by piece or step by step.

24 ★ Grow a Garden

Gardens represent life . . . beauty . . . health . . . nourishment. They reflect the seasons. They put you in touch with the great rhythms of life, growth, and death. Grow one! It will help you grow in esteem.

Flowers or vegetables, the choice is yours. Do all the work or only part of it. Do, however, make certain that you occasionally put your hands into the soil and touch the plants. Don't just watch your garden as a process from afar. Take an active part in its design, development, and cultivation.

Working in the earth and with plants does several things to build your self-esteem:

A garden puts you in touch with the Creator That is almost always a sure reminder of your status as a unique created being. Notice how each plant is different, how each flower has a slightly different character. Notice how different colors and textures blend together. Isn't the variety in your garden incredible? Reflect on your individuality and the ways in which you are distinctly different from, and yet capable of blending with, those around you.

A garden reminds you of the value of all living things
Everything within the natural world has a function and purpose. Human beings function in similar ways. Each of us has something within that is capable of nourishing others. You have beauty to give. You have talents that can blend with those of others and messages that are important to communicate to others.

A garden reminds you of many natural law and spiritual law principles You are confronted with the principle of a seed. Although you may plant it and water it, a power far greater than that of a human being actually causes the seed to grow. You are confronted with the fact of weeds and insect pests. Your life, too, is often plagued by unwanted intrusions. A garden encourages you that you can survive transplanting, pruning, and hard freezes.

A garden reminds you of your role as a steward of the earth You are a caretaker of the world around you.

A garden reminds you that nothing flourishes without nourishment and care Just as garden plants need water, sunlight, fertilizer, and daily care, so you must avail yourself of the nourishment you need.

A garden reminds you of the joys of the process
There's great pleasure in the planting and cultivating stages of life, not only the harvest.

25 ★ Don't Do It All

The person with low self-esteem often fails to delegate responsibilities or chores to others. He becomes so accustomed to thinking of himself as the "doer" that he willingly takes on all the less-than-elegant work of life without questioning whether it is truly his obligation or job.

This is not to say that any work is beneath the dignity of any person. All work has value, and all jobs have merit. It is to say that always being at the whim and command of others to do tasks outside one's job description is not characteristic of a person of healthy self-esteem. The person with healthy self-esteem is always willing to do whatever it legitimately takes to grow and achieve, but she isn't willing to be "used" by others.

Learn to Delegate (and to Delegate Fairly) If you supervise persons to whom you can pass on some jobs and responsibilities, do so. Give them jobs you don't mind doing as well as ones you don't like. Reward them for their efforts. Appreciate their contribution.

Guard Your "Volunteer" Time and Energy Is your plate already filled with church-related activities? Say no when you are asked to take on one more committee, no matter how worthy the mission. Is your schedule already filled to the max? Say no when you are asked to volunteer your time for the community project, no matter who asks you.

Say No When Asked to Do Anything Demeaning to Your Personhood Do you feel as if a "friend" is using you to run her errands and do her chores because she simply has failed to budget her own time and energy wisely? Politely but firmly say, "I can't help you right now." (If you lose her friendship over saying no, question whether she was really a friend in the first place.)

Childhood neighborhood bullies often seem to reemerge in the form of supervisors, spouses, colleagues, or fellow club members. There comes a time when it's best to say, "This is my neighborhood, too."

26 ★ Conduct a Language Audit

The person with low self-esteem often doesn't limit her negative thinking or negative comments to herself. She frequently becomes cynical about all of life, with a hefty side order of sarcasm and cutting criticism.

Listen to Yourself Conduct a language audit. Listen to what you say and how you say it. Use a tape recorder if you need to become more objective. Really "hear" yourself—both the words you use and the tone in which you speak them.

- Does your voice have a biting edge?
- Are you sarcastic?
- Do you project a cynical outlook on life?

Are you always suspicious of what you cannot see or do not know, always cautioning others against certain people or activities, always warning others not to take a risk?

- Do you frequently hear yourself pointing out another person's bad points?
- When you see a movie or play, read a book, or hear a performance, is your first response one of pointing out the good in it, or do you immediately zero in on what was wrong?
- Are you a complainer?
- Do you have a definition or criteria for determining when something is wonderful?

Most of us are far better at defining *awful* than we are at defining *marvelous*. It's easier for us to tell when we feel bad than when we feel good. It's easier for us to identify the missing piece, point out the error, or find the smudge on the piece of paper than it is for us to supply the missing piece, resolve the error, or clean up the mess.

Be a Truth Speaker Choose to become a truth speaker, which means communicating the whole truth about something, both good and bad. Choose to change your tone.

Change the way you speak about other people . . . about events and performances . . . about your work and that of others . . . about life! You'll change the way you think.

27 ★ Set a Deadline

The periodic down day, the trough of your biological rhythm chart, the bad circumstance that hits out of the blue—all are a part of life. Feeling momentarily down, however, shouldn't progress into a long-term outlook of poor self-esteem.

Choose a Date   Set a time when you put an end to the grieving.

Mark a moment when you choose to stop complaining about something.

Circle the date on the calendar when you are going to come out of mourning and attend the dance.

Choose a day on which you will become "available" again to date socially. If no one asks you to do something on that day, take the initiative and invite someone out to dinner or to a movie.

Move On   In so doing, you are activating a decision to move on in your life—to push your boat back into the main stream of the river. You are

putting yourself in a position to laugh again . . .
try again . . . create again . . . work again.

- Say to yourself after you are fired from your
job, "I lost that job. I failed at it. But I refuse to
let this convince me that I will always fail. I'll
allow myself to mourn all weekend, but on
Monday morning, I'm going to get up and
start beating the bushes in search of my next
opportunity."
- Say to yourself after the divorce, "I'm going to
give myself six months to heal and to grow.
And then I'm going to start inviting small
groups of people to do things with me or to
come over to my house for potluck dinners."

Talk to Others   At times, it is helpful to talk
to another person about what you need to do to
make amends for a failure or a mistake. The idea
of penance carries over into all areas of life. Accept
and define a "punishment" for yourself, and then
once you have completed that onerous chore, that
painful process, that job, or that payment schedule
—put the mistake behind you. Don't punish yourself for the rest of your life for an error.

At times, asking forgiveness of another person
and receiving forgiveness should mark the "end"
of the issue for you. Give the quarrel or the argument a definitive end. Shake hands at the end of
the fight. Reach a decision or a conclusion after a

debate. Decide that bygones really will be bygones.

A significant portion of low self-esteem can be attributed to continuing to hang on to things long after you should have let go of them—be it cutting comments, mistakes, sins, losses, or failures. Sound a bell in your soul to put an end to the round.

28 ★ Go Anyway

The person low in self-confidence generally doesn't enjoy being alone in a crowd. He'd rather be truly alone so that he can always define his rules and choose his outs.

Have Fun   Learn to go places by yourself and have fun with other people even if you don't arrive with them or leave with them. The only way to learn this is to do it.

Can't find anybody to go with you to the movie? Go by yourself. You may see someone there you know. If not, you'll at least view the movie that appeals to you.

What should you do if you're alone and a couple invite you to go to lunch with them after church? Go! Bon appétit!

Do you find yourself without a date for the club banquet only three days away? Go alone. There's so much mingling at most parties that many people may not even realize you arrived by yourself. Furthermore, once you're there, you'll find others who don't have dates, and they'll be grateful for someone to talk with. If you're bored or feel left out after you arrive, you can always leave early.

Pursue Your Interests Do you stay away from church because your family won't go with you? Go anyway.

Do you force yourself to go to the football game when you'd really rather be at the opera? Do you go to the ballet when you'd really rather stay at home and watch the tennis match? Find a way to compromise. Perhaps you can still buy season tickets to the opera for your wife and a friend, with the understanding that you're also buying a season pass to the football games for yourself and your friend's husband.

You don't need to share all of the interests of the other members in your family. You can go alone to the gallery, the museum, the shops. You can drive to the lake or hike in the mountains by yourself.

Some people fear that enjoying separate activities causes a rift in a relationship. That is rarely the case. Rifts tend to arise from other factors. Usually, two people who engage in separate activities find they have more to communicate about with each other. Both are happier doing what they enjoy doing, and their happiness rubs off on the relationship.

Guidelines In pursuing separate activities, follow some simple guidelines:

- Keep the communication lines open with your family members or those to whom you are committed in a relationship. Tell them where you are going, what you'll be doing, who you'll be going with (if anybody), and when you'll return.
- Don't exclude your spouse from the things you enjoy doing.
- Don't commit yourself to "side" relationships that might damage or destroy the family relationships to which you have already committed.

Learn to enjoy what gives you pleasure in life, even if you have nobody else to share it with at the moment. Don't blame someone else for the things you give up, or give someone else a hard time for not accompanying you to places or events to which you'd like to go.

When you learn to enjoy going places and doing things by yourself, you invariably gain self-esteem. You discover that you like going places with the person named *you!*

29 ★ Reward Yourself

Have you accomplished something worthwhile in your estimation, but nobody noticed? Have you finished a major project, but nobody applauded? Have you passed a milestone, but nobody congratulated you?

Reward yourself!

Buy yourself a present Perhaps it is something totally frivolous or indulgent. Maybe a new set of golf clubs or a make-over at a local salon.

Go on the trip of your choice Get away for the weekend. Escape on a cruise.

Take yourself out to dinner Enjoy being waited on.

Send yourself flowers This reward is especially appropriate if the unlauded success was at work. You can write yourself an enclosure card of congratulations and sign it "a fan." Keep coworkers guessing about the sender!

Take a day of vacation   Spend it in whatever way you choose.

Celebrate your success   There are only two rules to self-impose as you reward yourself:

1. Don't choose as a reward anything that will bring you harm or reverse the trend of your success. There's no point in rewarding yourself for a weight loss by eating a banana split. There's no good in spending a lot of money on a reward for yourself because you just got out of credit card debt.

2. Don't reward yourself in a way that causes harm to someone else. Don't be vindictive in rewarding yourself or do something to "undo" another person.

You don't need to wait for the end of a large task or long-term project to reward yourself. Sometimes interim rewards are helpful and motivating. For example, if you have embarked on a three-year course of study, reward yourself at the end of each year or each semester.

The task doesn't have to be something in the public arena. Perhaps you've had a goal for several years of cleaning out the garage. Reward yourself when the job is done!

You don't have to let anybody else know about your reward. You can savor your own sweet success all by yourself. On the other hand, you may want to invite others to celebrate with you. Let them know what you're celebrating, and invite them to come along as your guests. Be prepared to pay their way.

The goal you've reached may be in your daily routine. Do you regularly work out at a gym? Have you reached a weight goal (for your body or on a certain machine) or finally completed the number of laps you set as a goal for yourself (on the track or in the pool)? Reward yourself with an extra half hour in the sauna or whirlpool!

Celebrating your successes has two great benefits. First, the celebration underscores your success in a positive way in your own mind and memory. When you recall a celebration, you recall the success that evoked it and vice versa. You are reinforcing your own good behavior. Second, you are pointing out to others (in an unarrogant way) that you have accomplished something and that your achievement is worthy of notice.

30 ★ Learn a New Skill

Perhaps you feel as if you just aren't good at anything. Try learning a new skill.

Discipline   Learn from somebody who knows what he is doing, is good at the thing you want to learn, and is a good teacher. Learn from someone who will be patient with you as you learn, will encourage you, and yet will require you to practice and exercise discipline.

Physical Attributes   Avoid areas in which you do not have the physical attributes for success. If you have weak ankles and a bad back, you probably don't want to undertake ice-skating. You're likely to hurt yourself in a major way. If you have poor small motor skills, try learning something that requires large muscle coordination. If your hand-eye coordination is poor, don't choose a skill that requires it.

Aptitude Try a field in which you show some aptitude. Do you really like to work puzzles? Consider computers. Many computer programs require the same logic as solving puzzles. Are you good with your hands and very patient? A wide number of handcraft items and needlework projects require only those two traits.

Interests Choose an area in which you have a strong interest. Have you always wanted to be able to shoot a bow and arrow? Take archery! Have you always thought it would be fun to design your own clothes? Learn to sew. Do you enjoy trying new foods? Learn to be a gourmet cook, and have fun experimenting with herbs, spices, and special sauces.

New Ventures Learning a new skill may well lead to a new job or career. The people who succeed in their careers tend to like what they're doing, have an aptitude for what they're doing, have learned their job from a pro, and are physically capable of doing the job. You can join their ranks.

Acquiring a new skill builds up both self-esteem and confidence simultaneously.

31 ★ Let Go

Sometimes we find ourselves in self-defeating, self-destructive situations or relationships in which nothing we say or do is right, communication is completely warped, and the emotional pain and strain of the relationship keep us continually at the breaking point. In such cases, the most esteem-producing thing we can do is to "let go."

Has your boss made it clear that there's absolutely no chance you'll ever be promoted or given a raise? Move on!

Has a loved one stated definitively that it's over and moved on to a new relationship? Swallow hard, cry as much as you need to, but cut the tie.

Does a person continually belittle you, ridicule you, or nag you every time you come around? Stay away.

Tell the other person you are leaving Don't just disappear or waft away or fail to show up on a Monday morning.

State your reasons for going as clearly and unemotionally as possible   If you are feeling stunted or put down, say so: "I don't sense that I have the opportunity to grow. I need to feel free to succeed." If you have been rejected or wounded, tell how you feel: "I'm in a great deal of pain, and I need to leave in order to heal." The best thing you can do for the other person ultimately is to explain what has caused you the pain that you feel or to give the reason for your leaving.

Don't be talked out of going   If you hurt enough to leave in the first place, you are in sufficient pain to need some space and time to heal before reentering the relationship. Even if the person promises to make constructive changes in his or her life, he or she will need time to make those changes.

Don't assume that you'll never be back   You may want to leave the door open for reconciliation or a return. You may want to cite specific things that must be done in order for you to remain in contact or attempt to renew your relationship. If the time comes when you know that you will not be coming back permanently, let the person know that you won't be returning.

You may not be the one who needs to do the leaving. You may need to get rid of the employee, break off the relationship with the one you've dated for a long time, or ask another person to leave your home (spouse, grown-up child, even a stay-too-long visitor or relative). If so, adapt the same suggestions: tell the other person to leave and why, don't be talked out of your decision, and leave the door open for the person's return even as you temporarily change the locks.

Spinning around at the end of an emotional cul-de-sac causes you to lose your equilibrium, and it can destroy your confidence and self-esteem. Break the pattern. Walk away. Let go, or ask the other person to walk away.

Divorced people sometimes remarry.

Fired people are sometimes rehired by the company.

Relationships can heal.

Love is a renewable resource.

Still, when a relationship has been severely damaged, time and space are necessary for true, lasting healing to occur. Give yourself an opportunity to heal and to regain your balance. Give yourself the chance for your self-esteem to be restored.

32 ★ Take a Course

Keep learning. Chart a course that promotes life-long learning. Expect to be in the process of learning something new until the day you die.

Enroll in a course of study at a local college or vocational school, your church, or a community "open university."

You may not want to hassle with credits and grades. You can nearly always audit a course, which generally means that you pay a slightly lower fee and are exempt from taking tests and writing papers but are still expected to attend classes, keep up with reading assignments, and contribute your ideas in class discussions.

Benefits A course of study can . . .

• keep you mentally stimulated.

No matter what you're studying, or even how many times you've studied that subject before, you'll undoubtedly encounter new ideas from new people. Learning is a great "high."

- occupy time otherwise spent worrying or feeling depressed.

Engage your mind in a subject other than yourself and your problems!

- improve your communication skills.

The more you are called upon to defend an idea—verbally or in writing—the more confidence you gain in the information you know and your ability to express yourself.

- give you the needed information or skills for a new job or promotion.

Jobs and promotions tend to go to the person with the most information.

- help you become more disciplined.

In making time for reading, research, or study, you're likely to be forced to live by a tighter schedule and become more disciplined.

Accomplishment You'll have a sense of accomplishment upon completion of a course of academic study or vocational training.

33 ★ Shrug It Off

We often tease people about being Teflon coated. You know the type. No problems ever seem to stick to them as they sail smoothly through life. They never seem to be blamed for anything. That's never truly the case, of course. Everybody causes problems and has problems. The Teflon-coated analogy is a good one to use, however, when it comes to critical comments aimed at us. Sometimes we just need to let things slide off.

Disengage Yourself Is someone cursing at you because of a traffic tie-up for which you aren't responsible? Shrug it off.

Is a stranger shouting at you angrily for something he perceives you did? Do not take offense.

Is someone calling you names for no apparent reason? Refuse to be upset.

Don't let an idle angry, insulting, or derogatory comment stick to your soul or fester in your psyche.

Don't mentally rehearse the scene to yourself later.

Don't engage in an argument or hurl back insults.

You are not responsible for someone else's bad day or bad manners. Don't stand around and let someone unleash emotional steam in your direction.

Don't Take It to Heart   When someone who has lost emotional control lashes out at you in unrelated anger or frustration, don't let it ruin your day.

Don't take what the person says to heart.

Don't dwell on the words.

Don't use energy thinking up a clever quip or rebuttal.

Don't even give the words a second thought.

Don't let the person's bad day or bad self-esteem destroy how *you* feel about yourself or your day. If you do, you'll be basing your self-esteem and confidence on erroneous, incomplete information. Base your self-esteem only on what is spoken

- to you—yes, you specifically as opposed to you just because you happened to be standing nearby.
- in a calm, rational tone.
- truthfully—so that the message balances your faults against your good qualities.

34 ★ Take a Self-Defense Class

Do you feel powerless?

Do you feel scared in your own home?

Are you afraid to walk down the street by yourself?

If you live in a bad neighborhood, move! If your feelings of fear and powerlessness come from within, consider taking a self-defense class.

Learn how to prevent a crime against your person and property   You can reduce your chances of becoming a victim by learning some relatively simple techniques. In a self-defense class, for example, you can learn how to carry a purse or wallet and how to dress so as to discourage the casual pickpocket. You can learn safety tips, such as walking with someone else to your car in a poorly lighted parking garage and then driving that person to his or her car.

Learn how to protect yourself if you are attacked   Contact your local sheriff's office to learn where you can enroll in a self-defense class. You might also check with neighborhood organizations and community colleges.

Learn what to do to recover from an attack against your person or property Perhaps nothing is more damaging to one's sense of well-being and self-worth than to be attacked or injured. If you suffer such an experience, seek help. Don't allow the memories to overwhelm you. Don't assume that "you'll get over it" or attempt to dismiss the event as if nothing happened. Something *did* happen, and you won't be able to fool yourself into thinking otherwise; the emotions related to the experience, if unvented, will eventually explode. Get help that includes your family and spouse; you'll need their ongoing support, and in many cases, family members need assistance in handling their own feelings.

Learn how to handle verbal assaults Words do hurt, sometimes more than sticks and stones. A good self-defense course should include advice on how to handle the verbal assault as well as the physical one. If not, find a course specializing in that area.

In learning self-defense techniques you'll also gain the confidence that comes with information and rehearsal. You know what to do. You *can* handle a crisis. You *can* recover from one.

35 ★ Get Out of Debt

It's difficult to think positively about yourself if you're always dealing in negative numbers. Make a decision to get square with the world.

Map Out a Plan You may need financial counseling to help you learn how best to dig yourself out of the hole. One advisor suggests baking a credit-card cookie. He literally advises melting credit cards together and learning to live on a cash-only basis.

Put Yourself on a Timetable Set a date for paying off your personal indebtedness.

"But what about my house?" you might say. "It'll take me thirty years to pay off that one. Do I have to wait so long to improve my self-esteem?" Nah. In the first place, you might be able to refinance your house on a fifteen-year basis or add a couple of extra payments a year toward the principal, and save yourself several years and a bundle of cash in the process. Generally speaking, however, your house is an asset. It has value at tax time, and it's likely to appreciate in value.

Open a Savings Account and a Retirement Account

Even as you are reducing your debts, set aside a portion of money each month to add to the assets column in your ledger. Having money in savings sends a signal to your inner self: "Not only am I worth my weight in gold, but I've got some gold that's growing in weight!"

As you pay off your bills, add more to your savings account. Branch out into investments that are secure, perhaps government-secured certificates of deposit and high-quality stocks, municipal bonds, and so forth. Again, work with an expert.

Just imagine how good you will feel when the day arrives that

- you have no debts on which interest is accruing.
- all of your possessions are clearly your own.
- the mortgage on your home is paid in full.
- you have a substantial amount of money in savings, retirement accounts, and secure investments.

36 ★ Get a Job

Feeling out of the mainstream of society? Feeling as if nobody needs you—or needs you anymore? Find a job. Give it your best effort. Enjoy all its benefits!

Good Old-Fashioned Work Nothing dissipates a feeling of worthlessness (and the self-pity accompanying it) like getting a job. The advantages to your self-esteem are numerous.

The amount of money a person earns is not a true measure of character—not even a true indicator of value in society—but it is an indicator that the person is contributing toward his own good and the good of others. A job helps *you see yourself as part of the ongoing process* of a productive community.

Even if you volunteer your time and don't bring home a paycheck, you will see obvious ways in which *you are contributing to others*. If you aren't there, the job won't get done. Filling a niche says to your inner self, "I am needed. This job wouldn't have been done if I hadn't done it."

You are accountable to others—to persons on all levels of the organizational chart. In being accountable to others, you'll have a sense of responsibility to them and for them. Again, nobody fills that slot at any one time except you.

Having a job helps *you discipline other areas of your life.* It tends to make you more conscious of your communication skills. The better you communicate in the marketplace, the more others tend to respect you. The more they show respect, the more you tend to respect yourself.

You see progress in your life. Projects are completed . . . widgets are made . . . publications are printed and circulated . . . people are helped . . . clients or customers are satisfied . . . contracts are won. Sales charts show growth. Raises and promotions are awarded for good performance. New skills are acquired in the course of doing.

In having a job, you put yourself into a position where your personal growth in skills and your accomplishments can be more readily noted and rewarded by others—and if not by others, certainly by yourself!

37 ★ Have a Make-Over

Physical appearance has a direct impact on self-esteem. We all know the feelings we've had on a day when our hair just wouldn't lie down, we were "caught" without makeup, or we showed up at what we thought was to be a casual event way underdressed. We wanted to run and hide. And those feelings probably seeped into our broader self-perception, slightly contaminating our esteem and confidence.

Looking good directly relates to feeling good about ourselves.

Nearly all of us learn how to choose clothes, comb our hair, apply makeup or shave, and accessorize from our parents. But some of our parents didn't know much.

Others of us are still stuck in the look we had twenty years ago.

The moment comes for each of us when, as adults, we should avail ourselves of a professional make-over to best determine our own look. Start from scratch. Forget what you did in the past. Visit professionals and learn the following:

How to Do Your Hair   You may need to work with a stylist through several haircuts or even a few experiments with perms and color before you settle on the best look for you right now. Ask the stylist to show you some tricks and techniques you can use at home to achieve the look you want. Tell your stylist about the way you live—for example, if you travel a great deal, have nonstop days from the office to social events, or engage in lots of sporting activities. Let the stylist suggest a style appropriate for your activity level, your ability to work with your hair, your hair type, and the shape of your face. You may want to explore the world of wigs or toupees.

How to Apply Makeup   Insist the person teach you several looks: daytime professional, daytime casual, nighttime glamorous, and special techniques for times when you are to be photographed.

How to Dress   You may want to avail yourself of color analysis or proportional analysis. Many consultants now use computers to show you the way to achieve different looks or what you might look like in various styles. Have someone work with you who can help you pull a wardrobe together for maximum coordination and minimal expense. Learn the names of new types of garments. Ask questions of those who wait on you. Ask, "What goes with this?" "How do I wear this?"

"What do you suggest for my height and body shape?" Have your garments altered as necessary so that they always fit.

How to Accessorize Consider your eyeglasses to be your foremost accessory if you wear them. Learn how to choose items for correct proportion; watch others to see when certain types of jewelry, shoes, and purses are most appropriate. Get help in matching ties to suits and sportswear. Learn to tie scarves. Explore the world of hats.

Make fashion work for you in building up your self-esteem. Don't adopt a look just because it's the "in" thing. Adopt the look that's right for *you*. In so doing, you'll be able to face the world each day with an attitude of putting your best face forward!

38 ★ Try a New Experience

Do something you haven't done before. Try something you've always wanted to try. Explore a part of the world you've always longed to see.

Gaining new experience is a wonderful way for building up confidence that you can scout out and savor the world . . . and survive! The more successful fun experiences you have, the more you grow in a sense of self-value.

You need to follow only three guidelines in maximizing the self-esteem and confidence benefits that a new experience can afford you:

1. Choose something you *really want to do* Don't be talked into doing something or going somewhere just because everybody else is. Chart your own course.

2. Choose an activity or a trip that you can afford in terms of both money and time Debt and exhaustion are two experiences you can do without. (In fact, they are counterproductive to healthy esteem.)

3. Choose an activity in keeping with your moral code   Don't rebel against your value system. You'll experience guilt, and that's an experience unrelated to improved self-esteem and confidence.

If you've always wanted to learn to ballroom dance . . . sign up for the special set of free lessons now being offered.

If you've always wanted to learn to pilot a plane . . . save up your cash and take lessons.

If you've always dreamed of going to Paris . . . start mapping out a plan for getting there.

If you've always dreamed of taking a cruise ship to Alaska . . . start talking to your travel agent.

Don't assume that you'll go "someday." Someday rarely comes in time. Start setting dates and making plans. In some cases, the activity you dream of pursuing may require you to be in better physical shape than you're in today; start working out and getting ready.

New experiences build you up. They expand your horizons. They yield good material for musing, conversing, daydreaming, and remembering. They add to the substance of your thought life and build up your courage to take new risks in the future.

What's the new experience *you'd* like to try?

39 ★ Face the Scary Thing

Earlier we talked about facing your biggest fear—the feeling of being alone. The "scary thing" is not your biggest fear, but it can be a crippling fear. The scary thing is what causes panic to strike you in the pit of your stomach, your hands to go clammy, and your mouth to go dry.

Are you afraid

- of dogs?
- of flying?
- of driving?
- of spiders?
- of speaking to a group of people or even standing in front of a group of people?

Stunted Growth   Many times the fears that we acquire as children can haunt us all of our lives. Such fears stunt our growth in a certain area. When that happens, we are less confident as a whole than we can be or should be—and *without* any confidence in that one area of normal life and experience.

Conquered Fears Face up to the scary thing! Seek help in getting over it.

Work with someone who can help you overcome your phobia about dogs, birds, spiders, cats, bugs, or other creatures. You may not come to desire these animals as pets, but you can at least learn not to become hysterical when you find yourself in the same room with them!

Sign up for a "fear of flying" course. Several airlines now offer them.

Join Toastmasters. Learn to face people and speak your mind before them.

Are you scared of horses because one nibbled at you when you were seven years old? Take an equestrian class.

Are you scared to be around water because you never learned to swim? Learn to swim!

Are you scared to get back on a bicycle because you once had a terrible fall? Try again!

When you take on the scary thing and conquer it, you can't help experiencing a great burst of confidence and self-esteem. Where you were once lame, you're now able to walk. What cause for joy!

40 ★ Compliment Others

One of the best things a person with low self-esteem can do is to learn to compliment others. Very often the person of low esteem says to himself,

"I can't compliment others. It will take away from who I am, and I don't have anything to give away."

Or he says,

"I shouldn't compliment that person. I'm a nobody, and she's a somebody who doesn't need or want my compliment."

Both are false conclusions.

Give and Receive The more you compliment others, the more others will find something to compliment in you. The more they return your compliment (perhaps not immediately, but eventually), the more you will feel built up on the inside.

Everybody needs compliments. We can all use one more! In complimenting another person, you have the self-satisfaction of knowing that you have given something of benefit to another person. That sends a message to your inner self, "I am capable of giving to another person without losing. The good stuff inside me is more permanent than I thought."

Proper Delivery When you compliment others, keep these things in mind:

- Be genuine.

Speak sincerely. Don't say something you don't truly believe. Avoid using extremes, such as "greatest" or "most."

- Be discreet.

Don't make your compliment a show. You might want to write a note or speak to the person after all others have left his or her side.

- Be personal in your comments.

Say, "Your sermon really meant a lot to me because it caused me to think about some things in a new way," or "I laughed all the way through your skit; I needed a laugh today. Thanks for giving me one."

• Be brief and to the point.

You can always say simply, "Congratulations," or "I'm glad you won," or "I'm happy for you," or "Way to go." Don't overstate your case, take up too much of the person's time, or gush. Make your point and move on. A compliment shouldn't turn into an embarrassing moment for you or the person.

The person who imparts a blessing is an individual of inner strength of character. Imparting a blessing helps build that character even as it reflects it.

41 ★ Take an Aptitude or Personality Profile Test

You may be suffering from a lack of confidence and self-esteem stemming in part from your failure to discover the things for which you have innate talent and at which you have a great chance for success.

Aptitude Test One way to discover your talents is to take an aptitude test.

Most career planning or counseling centers at junior colleges or colleges can help you locate an appropriate test and may even be able to administer one to you. Employment agencies sometimes offer such tests, as do many private counselors and psychologists. You might also check with a minister at your church or the staff nurse or psychologist associated with your corporation.

Different tests evaluate different aptitudes and measure them in different ways, but generally speaking, you should be able to emerge from an aptitude test knowing more about your

- mechanical ability.
- creative ability.
- reasoning ability (logic).

Many tests can point you toward careers and jobs for which you are best suited as well as tell you basic aptitude strengths and weaknesses.

Personality Profile   Other tests are available to help you discover more about the way you relate to other people or project yourself to others. Myers-Briggs is perhaps the most famous of them.

It's comforting for many people to realize in taking these tests that they aren't better or worse than other people, only different. There's no such thing as a right set of aptitudes or a right personality. You possess a unique set of inherent abilities, likes and dislikes, and propensities. You show signs of your unique personality within hours after birth.

42 ★ Start Giving to Others

Seek to give your time and talents to help other people.

Visit the local Veterans Administration hospital to volunteer your services to those in rehabilitation.

Visit the local children's hospital. Volunteer to play games with the young patients.

Visit the local retirement center, especially the area in which the elderly are confined to their beds.

Visit the homebound who are members of your church.

Visit the Ronald McDonald house in your city.

Visit the homeless shelter.

Give Yourself As you get involved with individuals in need, you'll discover several things about them and about yourself:

- Everybody has something to give.
- Everybody needs somebody.
- Your help makes a difference—not only in

their lives but in your feelings of self-esteem.

Sometimes the problem you perceive in others is a problem they wouldn't dream of exchanging for the one they see in you!

Concentrate on Individuals Don't volunteer to help the masses. Seek to help only one or two people. Call them by name. Get to know them. Find ways in which you can help bring out their distinct gifts and traits. Don't seek to help humanity. Seek to help a human being.

Reach Potential Don't volunteer for service out of pity. Volunteer because you truly want to help another person enjoy a better quality of life and reach more of her human potential. Consider it a by-product that you'll also be growing and reaching more of your potential. The more you give, the more you get back.

43 ★ Adopt an Older Person

We need someone older and wiser in our lives to guide us, help us and, above all, affirm us. For many of us, those older and wiser people are our parents and grandparents. For others of us, our parents may have been older but not wiser. The person with low self-esteem frequently has parents who gave faulty guidance, meager help or help of the wrong kind, and little or no affirmation.

If you do not have someone older and wiser in your life, make friends with such a person. The person need not be all that much older than you in years. The person may simply be more knowledgeable or more experienced than you are.

Seek Out Older People Find ways to help your older friends; encourage them and spend time with them. Really get to know them. Go places together. Share experiences. Engage in lengthy life-sharing conversations. Ask their advice; draw from their wisdom. Appreciate what they have to share with you, and express your gratitude to them.

Seek Out a Mentor   Choose someone with the same interests or beliefs as yours. You may have several mentors for different areas of interest or career pursuit. Align yourself with someone who is willing to help you, makes himself available to help, and is affirming of who you are and who you can be.

Seek Out a Teacher   A mentor is someone who can guide you in making decisions and personal choices. A teacher is someone who shares information with you or teaches you a skill. If you want to learn something, find the best qualified person you can and study under him or her.

Sometimes a mentor is a teacher and vice versa —but sometimes not. Sometimes a teacher can become a mentor or a friend. Choose to be a good student, and your teacher will not only be a better teacher but a teacher of "life" beyond the subject specialty.

In having an older friend, a mentor, a teacher . . . you'll have an older person who is on your side. You'll be involved with someone who sees a bigger picture of life than you see and will affirm traits in you that no peer can recognize. You'll have someone in your life who is eager to cheer you on, prod you on, and push you to the full limits of your capability.

44 ★ Keep a Personal Journal

Keep a record of your life. Record moments of importance to you. Write of your successes. List, for your future reference, your

- dreams—about how you'd like your life to be.
- goals—what you'd like to do, see, accomplish, or produce.
- likes and dislikes.

A Daily Diary Keeping a daily diary sends a message to your inner self: "My life is important to me. What happens to me and through me is worthy of note."

Record your thoughts and feelings, not only what you do. Record dialogues of significance, writing in detail the "he saids" and "she saids."

Annual Reflection Consider spending a few hours at the end of each year reflecting on the previous twelve months and writing in some detail about the year's highlights. Write about relationships and encounters that have held special meaning for you, and tell why. Explore the struggles you have had, and draw some conclusions about them.

Lists Consider keeping a log of movies you see, books you read, handcraft projects you complete, gifts you give, trips you take, cultural events you attend. Not only will you find that a handy reference in planning future gifts and projects (or in recommending good movies and books to others), but you'll have an obvious objective source to check about what has been the input into your soul. Write a brief description next to each entry, telling what you liked most about it or what it meant to you.

Make lists occasionally about things you like and don't like, problems you're facing and how you plan to solve them, and new ideas. Getting your ideas and opinions down on paper can help you focus them and develop them.

Keep your New Year's resolutions or long-range goals in a place where you can refer to them periodically—perhaps at the back of your diary or journal. Check on your progress from time to time. Set new goals as you reach old ones.

Personal Profile Write down in your journal how you perceive yourself. List the things that you want to "be"—the traits you want to have in your life. Identify your foremost goals. Put into words what you perceive to be your purpose for being. When you are feeling down, consult your journal. Read again about the person you are and the person you aspire to be. Never forget that you *are* your goals and dreams as well as your past accomplishments.

A personal journal is *your* reference tool. Write to yourself and for yourself. You'll undoubtedly find that you enjoy reading about yourself from time to time! In that, you're developing healthy self-esteem.

45 ★ Get It Fixed or Accept It

Do you avoid smiling because your teeth are crooked or discolored?

Do you hate going out in public because you think everyone is staring at your nose?

Do you feel too fat—or too thin—to be lovable?

Do you avoid getting too close to people because you fear you will offend them in some way?

Do you feel sorry for anyone wearing glasses because you feel sorry for yourself that you do?

Do you hate the fact that you're going bald to the point you are starting to hate yourself?

Fix the problem!

Professional Assistance See your dentist, doctor, ophthalmologist, or dermatologist. You may be able to do something about that annoying physical attribute for less money and in less time than you thought. Braces may be an option. Contact lenses may be a solution. You may want to explore the possibility of dental or cosmetic surgery. You may want to talk to your doctor about hair transplants.

At the same time, do some soul-searching with a professional counselor. Explore why and how your outer appearance is affecting your inner self. Talk over the problems you perceive your physical appearance is creating for you. Reappraise your desire for personal beauty and your expectations about how much you can change your appearance. Reevaluate what you hope to achieve through changes in your appearance.

No Excuses Face the fact that you cannot change some things about yourself. You aren't likely to grow or shrink in height, for example. Change what you can change without causing yourself harm, and learn to accept what you cannot.

Don't subject yourself to unnecessary surgery. Every surgical procedure has some risks and some potential negative side effects. Seriously weigh whether you need to "cut and paste" your face or body to achieve your goal of an acceptable appearance.

Quit complaining about your physical appearance. Work on it, do what you can, and then go with it. Don't continually call attention to what you perceive to be a weakness.

Stop using your physical appearance as an excuse for not participating, not joining in, not going. Stop using your physical appearance as a justification for not succeeding or not trying.

By Any Other Name Some people cringe every time anyone calls their name or nickname. If you are one of those people, see an attorney—or consult with a librarian—about how you can change your name legally. Have your business cards reprinted with the name you desire to have. Start signing your name to Christmas cards the way you want others to address a card to you. Send a signal to your friends that you no longer answer to a nickname. Your name is your name! Even though it was given to you by someone else, it's within your grasp to change it if you don't like it.

46 ★ Don't Let Others Bring Up the Past

Perhaps nothing is more annoying or more damaging to one's attempts at rehabilitative self-esteem than to have another person continually bring up a past failure, hurt, or loss.

Responses When you encounter a person who attempts to bring up something that you have already forgiven and would rather forget, declare,

- "I'm sorry, but I'd really rather not talk about the divorce. I'm trying to move forward in my life and take things as they are and can be, not as they were or as I might wish they were."
- "I appreciate your concern, but that's in my past now. I know God has forgiven me for that, and I've tried hard to forgive myself and every other person involved. I hope you can forgive them and me, too, and help me to put this in my past."
- "I'm trying to remember only the good times."

- "That was then. This is now. I'm really liking now a lot better."
- "I know that's a part of my history, but I'm concentrating now on creating a better future."

More Than Crises   Sometimes the people who bring up the past are attempting to do so to show you that they are your allies. They are trying to be on your side. At other times, the people simply don't know what else to talk to you about! (Many times, a divorce, death, or other major injury to self-esteem seems to be the number one topic of conversation for so long, we forget—and so do others—that we have other interests and facets to our lives.)

Accept their interest in you, and extend appreciation for their friendship. At the same time, change the subject to something that you both have shared or might share. Show your interested friends that you have more to your life than a painful incident or major crisis. In showing them, you'll reinforce the idea to yourself!

47 ★ Attempt One Major Change at a Time

Certain events in life knock us for a loop, whether we want them to or think they will. Death. Divorce. Loss of a business or job. The empty nest. The mid-life panic attack. Menopause. A move to a new city. Retirement. Marriage. A first job. A first child. Numerous are the "big events" of our lives, and they invariably involve change.

The Big Events   As far as is possible, attempt only one major change in your life at a time. You'll have a much better chance to succeed at it and thereby regain your self-esteem balance and achieve confidence in the new area, group, or skill. For example, avoid starting a new job and a new marriage at the same time, or avoid getting a divorce during a mid-life crisis.

Unfortunately, following divorce or death, many people find themselves a single person, a single parent, and a sole breadwinner simultaneously and immediately. That's all the more reason for establishing a strong support group of friends from whom you can ask help. Nobody can handle that many changes at one time all alone.

On a Smaller Scale Not only should you avoid tackling more than one major change in life at a time, but you should avoid the following:

Avoid trying to change more than one bad habit at a time Try making only one major New Year's resolution at a time. Trying to change too much about yourself overnight is a setup for failure!

Avoid joining more than one new group at a time Instead, set the goal of getting to know the people in that first group at a deeper level.

Avoid attempting to achieve more than one major goal at a time Think "sequence" instead of "concurrent" as you attempt to make changes in your life.

Avoid trying to concentrate on more than one major project at a time You'll invariably find yourself thinking about one just when you should be thinking about the other.

Avoid attempting to volunteer for more than one group at a time Being committed in too many places or to too many people generally means that you will be spreading yourself too thin to be successful or to enjoy what you're doing. The key issue here is the extent of your commitments and the time each one requires. You may find that you can juggle several small time commitments.

Attempting too much at one time throws your entire system out of whack, and rather than succeed at one of your goals, you're likely to fail at all of them. That becomes a real blow to your self-esteem and confidence, just when you thought you were in the process of growth, self-improvement, or getting healthy again!

48 ★ Renew Your Vision for Your Life

You may become so caught up in the daily routine that you forget the big picture. Take time periodically to recall *why* you are doing what you are doing . . . *where* you set out to go (figuratively speaking, but in some cases, literally speaking, too) . . . and *how* you truly want to order your days and spend your hours.

Probing Questions Ask yourself two sets of questions:

> *What did I really want to do when I was a child?*
> *What did I enjoy playing the most as a child?*

Very often, the person's childhood vision for life and the childhood activities most enjoyed come very close to revealing the person's primary talents, aptitudes, and desires. For example, it's not uncommon for the little boy who desired to be a fireman to have a great aptitude for being a personnel agent or a customer relations employee who can "put out the fires" of crisis in another person's life. (A big red car is optional.)

The child who enjoyed playing with paper dolls, dressing and redressing them with different accessories, making new clothes for them, and designing environments for them often has an excellent aptitude for entering the world of fashion retailing or some area of design (fashion designing, interior decorating, graphic art, and so forth).

What do I consider to be an ideal day?

The way a person envisions a "perfect day" often reveals priorities. The ideal day is nearly always more relaxed in pace and has more human contact and satisfying communication than the present.

Stop to consider your ideal day for a moment. And then ask yourself a related question: *What do I need to change about my schedule, agenda, and the way I live in order to have more ideal days?* (Bear in mind that nobody can live an ideal life. You can, however, forge the frequent ideal day!)

Readjustment Use these questions to begin a conversation with your spouse. If you live alone, write down some of your answers to these questions. You'll likely find yourself coming to decisions about how you can readjust your daily schedule, make alterations in your time commitments, and set new goals (which may include going back to school or entering a new area of training). At the root of your vision for your life are your priorities —those things you decide are most important to you—and your values, the system of beliefs by which you establish priorities.

Reinstituting your values and setting new priorities based on them can lead to personal growth.

49 ★ Spend Time with Children

In spending time with young children, you'll be in the roles of teacher, helper, and doer.

Free to Play If you'll allow yourself the freedom to get down on the floor and play with children (at what they want to play), you'll be in the role of a cocreator and senior playmate.

All of these roles can build up your self-esteem. It's a fabulous feeling to have a two-year-old declare, *"I like playing with you; you're fun,"* or ask, *"Can you come over again real soon?"* or report, *"I helped do this; he showed me how!"*

Free to Renew Curiosity When you enter a child's world—really get down on the child's level and explore life with him—you put yourself in a position to renew your sense of play, wonderment, curiosity. You're likely to get back in touch with feelings and ideas that have been long since buried. And all of that can be restorative therapy for your self-esteem.

Children have a great capacity for taking risks.

Let a little of their "fearless" attitude rub off on you and enhance your confidence.

At times, association with children may dredge up hurtful memories; your friendship with a child may conjure feelings of lost innocence or evoke a desire to spare the child the pain you knew. Spare the child a description of your pain. Explore those feelings on your own or with a helpful adult. Seek healing for those bad times in your childhood.

No matter what type of childhood you had, you can always approach a small child with the intention: "I want to help you have a better childhood than I had. I want to help you see more of the world, experience more joy, explore more of your own abilities and ideas, laugh more, and establish an even greater vision for who you can be than you would otherwise experience without me." In adopting that perspective as you deal with a young child, you will also be calling forth that perspective in your life. Your self-esteem and confidence will be rejuvenated.

50 ★ Vow a Better Vow

We don't have a mechanism in our culture for "undoing" a vow after it's made. Our intentions and commitments are rarely undone in a ceremonious, helpful, or hopeful manner that is equitable and beneficial to all parties involved. We *break* our promises. We *break* hearts. We *break* up families or associations. We *break* off communication. In the process, we break a part of who we are.

The only way out of a broken vow is to make a better one.

The Standard A "better vow" looks toward the future and sets a higher standard. It replaces the previous vow, not negating the value of the one broken but expressing a desire rooted in hope and determination that the future will bring healing and greater strength.

Generally speaking, make the better vow in yourself and for yourself. Don't vow to do something because someone else is insisting that you make a vow or nagging you to do so. You'll inevitably break such a vow. Make only those vows in which you require something of yourself—usually something more or something better. Then, value yourself enough to fulfill the vow you've made to yourself!

The Commitment Don't make a public declaration of commitment or intention unless you are 100 percent serious about pursuing that commitment and are determined with maximum determination that you are going to do *whatever* it takes to fulfill your new obligation—including doing things you may find painful or difficult. For example, don't vow to your child that you'll never miss another major performance in his life if you aren't willing to tell your boss no when he asks you to attend the Friday night training session.

The Positive Keep your vows positive. Don't say to yourself, "I'm never going to get another divorce." Say instead, "When I remarry, I vow to give my marriage my utmost effort and make it my highest priority relationship."

Don't make a vow that impinges upon or negates one you've already made and to which you are still committed. In other words, don't use a "new vow" to undermine one still in effect or to break an existing vow. For example, don't vow to a partner that you're going to give your best ideas and energy to a part-time enterprise if you've already made a vow within yourself to succeed at your full-time job and be the best employee your company has!

The Attainable Finally, don't make your "better vow" lightly. Weigh your past failures. Seriously evaluate your desire and ability to make certain changes. Undertake only the vows that you realistically can expect to keep. Commit only to what you believe is attainable. For example, don't vow to yourself that you're going to do whatever it takes to become an Olympic swimmer if you're presently fifty years old!

Vows are the most serious declarations you can make to others and to yourself. Take them seriously. Do what it takes to fulfill them. When you break one, replace it with a better vow. In making and keeping vows, you'll undergird your self-esteem in a way that nothing else can.

51 ★ Ask God's Help

Turn to your Creator for a sense of your identity. He fashioned you. Trust Him to be able to

- show you a way of restoration.
- reveal to you a path of deliverance.
- heal what is sick . . . mend what is broken . . . and restore what is injured.
- help you identify areas in which you need to make changes, and give you the energy and willpower to make them.
- put back together the shattered pieces of your life.
- cleanse your memories and free you from guilt.
- show you who He created you to be.

Admit to your Creator that you are wounded . . . inadequate. Ask God to help you.

Rely on the Divine Helper   There's only so much you can do to build your self-esteem and confidence. There's only so much that others can do to help you. Avail yourself of divine wisdom and strength. He who created you knows everything about you, including your full potential. Explore who you are as a human being fashioned by Him. Aim at all you can be, as He has uniquely made you.

II. Build Your Child's Self-Esteem and Confidence

To
Jeff and Christi
with love

Contents

■ Preface

Parenting is tough work. It takes wisdom, daily diligence, and a heart filled with patience. There's nothing "simple" about raising a child.

There are, however, some fairly simple parenting skills and methods that can make the process more fun, the responsibility more manageable, and the results more effective. This section offers over fifty suggestions for building your child's self-esteem and confidence.

Your child's self-esteem is rooted in an understanding of his or her *value*, especially his or her value as perceived and conveyed by you. No one can instill self-esteem in a child as well as a loving parent. Your child needs to know the reality of your love and that you count him or her as priceless. In order for your child to grow into an emotionally healthy adult, make the formation of your child's self-esteem one of your top parenting priorities.

Your child's self-confidence is rooted in an understanding of his or her abilities. Children need to believe that they can cope with failure, achieve positive goals, and handle themselves with ease in a variety of situations. It is by watching you, listening to you, and following your lead that your child will learn essential life-skills. In the training of your child make the building of self-confidence one of your main goals.

A child who is confident and has high self-esteem is a child who strives for, and comes closest to reaching, his or her full potential. A child with self-esteem is a child who believes in his or her own capacity to grow and adapt. And that is a child with hope!

As a loving parent, you can learn and employ simple techniques in the course of everyday living that will help build your child's self-esteem and confidence. The job is do-able. And you are capable. Value yourself. Have confidence in your own ability to parent. That's step number-one toward modeling positive self-esteem and self-confidence for your child.

Believe in yourself and in your child, and your child will believe you and believe what you have to say.

1 ■ Learn and Employ The Art of Compliment

A child thrives on frequent praise and recognition. Watch a child receive genuine and heartfelt words of approval from a respected adult—be it parent, grandparent, teacher, or pastor—and you can almost see that child grow an inch on the inside.

"Way to go!"

"Good job!"

"I'm very proud of you."

A child should be praised for awards received, good grades earned, or games won. A word of praise may be considered a "verbal trophy." A child's psyche has abundant shelf space for such honors.

A child should also be praised for behavior that represents a struggle and victory from the *child's* perspective. "I'm proud of you for sitting so quietly in church, today. I know it was tough to do, but you did it!"

A child should be praised for behavior the parent wants to see again! "I know you must have wanted to say something when she screamed at you, but I'm proud of you for keeping your cool." Such compliments are nearly always related to a particular achievement or a specific behavior.

Can we assume, then, that all compliments and words of praise build a child's self-esteem?

To the contrary, not all praise-giving has a positive effect. Here are some guidelines for the use of compliments and praise.

Your praise must be sincere. Don't say something if you don't really mean it. Adults resent insincere compliments and children do, too. Telling your daughter five times a day, "You're so cute," is likely to be regarded by your child as meaningless. After a while, your child may think she always looks cute (even when she doesn't) or that you are blind.

True praise is best expressed privately. Don't grandstand. Let your child know in a special one-to-one moment how you feel.

Praise your child for those things that you both regard as important.

For praise to be received as praise, the adult must be perceived as *sharing* the child's delight at the child's accomplishment.

Genuine, heartfelt praise for worthy accomplishments has no substitute in building a child's self-esteem and confidence. Praise is one of the building blocks for establishing a child's sense of self-worth, and it encourages a willingness to try new activities and more difficult goals.

2 ■ Don't Allow Your Child to Be Self-Critical

In building self-esteem, a child's criticism of his or her own actions is acceptable. Criticism of "self" is not.

Watch your child's responses when he or she experiences failure. These actions will tell you a lot about your child's level of self-esteem.

"I'm just a dummy," said Kevin after he lost five successive games of tick-tack-toe. "Dummy, dummy, dummy."

Kevin learned those negative responses from someone, somewhere, at some time. The sadder implication, however, is that Kevin has started equating his performance in one area of life with his value as a human being. He was not only criticizing his performance, he was criticizing himself. At that point a parent or other caring adult needs to step in.

A few months ago, I witnessed a phenomenal event. I saw Rob swing and miss at forty-eight consecutive pitches from an automatic ball-pitcher at the local batting range. Several friends and a couple of adults stood nearby offering encouragement, advice, cheers when he came close, and dismay when he missed by a mile. Eleven-year-old Rob had lots of witnesses for his forty-eight swings. Six rounds at twenty-five cents each and not one hit! Not even a foul ball.

He didn't seem remotely concerned. "Tough deal," I said as he walked out of the cage.

"Yeah," he said as he sat down beside me. "I've been trying for two years to hit one. I can hit the softball pitches," he added matter-of-factly. "And I can hit about half the slow-speed pitches. But I haven't got any of the medium-speed ones, yet."

Two years. I couldn't get over the fact that Rob had tried and failed for two years to hit a medium-speed pitch. He must have swung at several thousand balls hurled at him from that unseen machine. Furthermore, he displayed no intent to give up. Everything about his attitude said he'd be at that range every weekend until he mastered the medium-pitch.

I was equally impressed with the fact that Rob could be so matter-of-fact about his failure. He certainly didn't consider himself "stupid" or "dumb" for missing those pitches—not even in the presence of friends and family.

"But, children do make mistakes," you may say. "They do perform badly. Isn't it wrong to ignore errors?"

Yes, children fail. In fact, they often fail at a task many more times than they succeed. A child's failures at certain tasks, however, do not mean that the child is a failure as a child!

What are some positive responses that an adult can make when a child acknowledges failure?

"Did you hear me miss that chord?" said Rachel after

a single flub in an otherwise flawless piano recital performance. "I really blew it."

"Yes," I agreed. "You blew four out of 1,302 notes. Pretty good percentage, I'd say." Rachel might not even know what "percentage" means, and I wasn't certain there were 1,302 notes of music in the piece she played. The point was, we both knew she failed at one small part of one task, and that it was incidental to her personal worth.

"I couldn't hit the side of a barn today," said Jeff after being removed from the pitcher's mound in the sixth inning. "A small barn or a big barn?" I asked. He grinned. We both knew he had experienced an off day, yet we wouldn't let this setback diminish his self-image.

Sure, kids err. They can and should acknowledge their mistakes, but we must make certain they keep their self-criticism limited to the realm of actions, not of self.

When adults allow children to criticize themselves they think, *You agree with me. I must really be stupid. I must really be a dummy.* Allowing your child to transfer an unsuccessful performance into a negative sense of self-worth prompts the thought, *You think my worth as a person is tied up in my ability to perform well."*

Both conclusions can destroy self-esteem, if they go uncorrected. No child should be allowed to criticize *who* he or she is, and never should a child be allowed to equate mistakes or failure to self-worth.

3 ■ Please and Thank You—Both to and from Your Child

Good manners are not only a subject for parents to teach children. They are actions for parents to *show* children.

Do you say "Please" when you make a request of your child? Do you say "Thank you" to your child (not just for gifts, but when your child follows through on requests you have made)? Or are you requiring behaviors of your child that you rarely model?

If you want your child to have good manners, display good manners to your child. Your child has an inborn ability to mimic your behavior, and the easiest way to teach good manners to children is to model them on a daily basis.

"Please" and "Thank you" aren't just for Sundays or formal outings. Use them when your child passes the butter at the dinner table and helps carry the groceries in from the car.

Your display of good manners says to your child, "I value you as much as I do the stranger in the market who gets a 'thank you' when she tells me where I can find the lima beans."

Your display of good manners says to your child, "I

want you to be able to move adeptly at all levels of society and to respect and treat with tact all types of people."

As one parent told her son, "I want you to be able to talk to any person as if you were talking to the president, because you may meet the president someday!" This parent obviously felt her son *worthy* to be in the president's company and that her child had value far beyond his immediate social standing. This mother was giving her child a glimpse into his own potential, even as she was building the self-esteem he would need to reach that potential.

- "Please."
- "Thank you."
- "I had a very nice time."
- "Pardon me."

Those four little phrases should become a seamless part of a child's confidence in facing strangers and working with others. When your child is an adult, good manners will soften your son or daughter's pride when dealing with coworkers and subordinates. Good manners will give dignity to your child's presence in any crowd. Give to your child the feeling that he or she is worthy of *your* best manners.

4 ■ Let Your Child Be "Child for a Day"

When was the last time you and your child had a special day together? Just the two of you?

Not just five minutes together before bedtime but an entire day, or at minimum, an entire afternoon or evening.

Not a time spent doing something routine but a time of doing something special.

Four times a year—or at least once every six months—make a "date" with your child. Plan a day, afternoon, or entire evening together. It may be a time devoted to making something, going someplace, or playing games together. Let your child help plan the event.

Craig takes Jeff to baseball games in Los Angeles, 120 miles from their home. It takes most of a morning to get to the park, stopping on the way for waffles with whipped cream and fruit. It takes all evening to get home, by way of rush-hour traffic and Burger King. Along the way, there's plenty of time for talk, or no talk. It doesn't matter, either, if the Dodgers win or lose. Craig and Jeff are together doing something they both enjoy.

Lynn takes Amy to a lookout café on sunny winter

afternoons to play monopoly. The tourist season is over so there's rarely anyone there. They order pizza and then spend all afternoon playing monopoly in the corner booth overlooking the valley. Amy loves to play monopoly. She also loves the hot fudge sundae that comes at the end of the game (no matter who wins). Lynn leaves a generous tip. "I'm paying more for rent than service," she says. It's an afternoon for talk, laughs, fun, and memories.

Both Craig and Lynn unwittingly but wisely follow the three main rules for planning a date with your child:

- Choose an activity your child enjoys.
- Choose a special activity that isn't an everyday event.
- Make a time for just the two of you to be together.

Special times like these say to a child, "I like you. In fact, I like being with you so much that I'm willing to take a whole day just for you."

For several years, Janice took one day of vacation from work each summer just so she and her daughter could go to the park or museum together. "I'd reach the point where I was *homesick* for time with my child," says Janice. "I wanted to be with Kimberly so much I knew I wouldn't be able to concentrate at work. I called it our 'goof-off' day."

What is one of Kim's favorite memories of her childhood? Goof-off days with Mom!

5 ■ Let Your Child Help Make Decisions

One of the most important skills your child will ever acquire is the ability to make sound decisions. Making decisions with care and integrity may well be the foremost skill required for creating a life marked by fulfillment, success, and satisfying relationships. It is also the decision-maker who propels our society forward. It is the decision-maker who assumes leadership.

Decision-making is not rooted in the ability to "think up" choices. Most adults rarely have the option of deciding all aspects of a circumstance, event, or relationship without limitations or restrictions of any kind. Nearly all adult decisions are influenced by such factors as budget, time, space, availability of resources, and the wishes of others. We do a disservice to a child when we ask him or her to face open-ended possibilities.

So, how do we help a child develop decision-making skills?

Give your child a closed set of options. "Do you want to buy this present or that one for your brother's birthday?" "Do you want to eat at McDonald's or Wendy's?" "Do you want to go bowling or ice skating on Saturday?"

Encourage your child to play games that require decision-making. Checkers, chess, board games, team sports, and other games are opportunities for children to learn to make decisions without parental influence.

Talk about the options your child chooses. "Looking back, do you think that was really the best move?" "What do you think was the turning point of the game?" "If you had it to do over again, would you have made the same choice?"

Stick to the child's choice. Once your child chooses an appropriate option, insist he or she stay with it. No waffling. No changing one's mind midstream. No backing out. Let your child experience the fact that every choice has a consequence.

Expand the number of options as your child develops decision-making skills.

Anticipate the day when your child will be able to choose from three, four, and many more options. "You may go to any one of these four movies this afternoon." Or, "You may choose any of the books on this library shelf to read."

Encourage your older child and teen to recognize the decision-making process at work.

One of the hallmarks of self-confidence is the ability to define options and to make a choice. One of the factors in the building of self-esteem is the ability to make a choice one is happy with as time passes!

6 ■ Give Your Child Swimming Lessons

One of the most confidence-building skills you can teach your child is the ability to swim.

Children who know how to swim overcome one of life's most gripping fears: the fear of water. Adults who don't know how to swim often are terrified to be out on boats, or even to fly over water. They may panic every time they see a child or animal near or in a swimming pool. Not knowing how to swim can be emotionally crippling and socially limiting.

In learning to swim, your child will not only overcome a major fear, but he or she will master a new skill and enjoy a new sense of physical coordination. Your child will learn, in the process, that fears can be faced, new skills can be acquired, and new levels of independence are possible. Your child will also learn that water safety techniques can prevent accidents.

How old should a child be before he or she is given swimming lessons?

Many parents begin to teach their child simple water-movement skills when the child is as young as six-months old. If you opt to begin this early, make certain you work with an instructor who is trained and experienced in teaching infants. The average age to begin swimming lessons is three- to four-years old, when a child has enough large-muscle motor skills to coordinate the basic arm and leg swimming motions. As soon as your child can "flutter kick," your child can learn to swim!

If, however, your child is a teen and he or she still doesn't know how to swim, don't assume it's too late. Run, don't walk, to the nearest YMCA or Red Cross swimming course!

How should you choose an instructor?

Make sure the instructor has Water Safety Instructor certification with the Red Cross. This ensures that your child's instructor not only has studied how to teach swimming, but that he or she has successfully taught swimming.

What should a child know how to do?

Make certain that the instruction includes water safety lessons, especially those related to boating safety and basic lifesaving and resuscitation techniques.

Make certain your child sticks with swimming lessons until he or she can float, swim twenty-five yards without stopping, and tread water for five minutes.

Make certain your child learns how to rub out leg cramps, when and how to dive, and how to keep his or her eyes open under water. (Many children seem to finish swimming lessons without acquiring these basic skills, which could make the difference between life and death in lake and boating accidents.)

A child should also be taught that swimming is fun,

but not a time for reckless abandon. Children need to be disciplined for disobeying swimming safety rules.

Finally, evaluate your own swimming skills.

Isn't it time you learned to swim if you don't know how? Isn't it time to take a refresher course in lifesaving techniques? Have you ever taken a CPR course?

The wise parent acquires the skills to be a child's number-one lifeguard whenever the child is near or in the water. To that end never let the child swim alone or unobserved. When your child is in the water, you should be watching from solid footing. When you are near water, bear in mind that water becomes a temptation to a child that enjoys swimming. Watch your child like a hawk.

Diedre, a mother of a two-year-old, went into the house to take a phone call. She came within seconds of losing her son, who had been playing with a ball twenty feet away from their swimming pool. When the ball rolled into the pool, Jeremy followed and fell in. Quickly performed CPR techniques made the difference between life and death.

Knowing how to swim is an important skill for children. It's an ability that builds confidence and self-esteem, and it can save your child's life.

7 ■ Make Your Child the Guest of Honor

Nothing makes a person feel more important than being elevated to the position of "guest of honor" by those he or she loves and values.

"You are cordially invited," read the elegantly handwritten invitation, "to a dinner in your honor."

This was the message on a ribbon-tied scroll handed to Jamie when he arrived home from soccer practice.

The reason for the honor? Jamie's excellent report card had arrived in the mail earlier that day. It was the best report card Jamie had ever earned; it marked the successful conclusion of a period of serious study and hard-to-come-by concentration on homework assignments, a major feat for a boy who would rather be kicking a soccer ball than studying history.

To mark the event, Jamie's mother brought out the family's best china, crystal, and silver from the dining room cabinets. She set the table with linens and candelabra. She fixed Jamie's favorite foods: hot dogs, potato chips, baked beans, and chocolate cake. Hot dogs on a silver platter? You bet. Potato chips in a crystal bowl? Absolutely.

Jamie's father offered a "toast" at the beginning of

the meal. With apple-juice-filled glasses, Jamie's brother, mother, and father, all raised their glasses in honor of Jamie. His father gave a little speech and mentioned Jamie's excellent report card during the blessing before the meal began.

The message of the evening was brought home clearly with a two-line conclusion to the meal from Jamie's mother: "Special accomplishments deserve special recognition, Jamie. We're proud of your special accomplishment."

(Jamie, of course, didn't have to help clear the table or load the dishwasher, which may have been his favorite part of the entire event).

According to Jamie twenty years later, that evening was one of his most satisfying childhood experiences. "It was the first time I realized I could accomplish something that other people openly acknowledged as important. It was a growing-up point."

Of course a parent need not go to such lengths to make a child feel special. Betty has a family heirloom plate that she positions occasionally at one of her children's established places at the dinner table. The appearance of that plate signifies a reward, and the dinner menu includes one or more of the child's favorite dishes. The most recent occasion? A no-cavity report from a visit to the dentist's office.

A child's self-esteem—the understanding that he or she has value and worth—is built up every time a child is recognized as special and counted as important.

8 ■ Ask Your Child's Opinion

A big part of a child's self-esteem is rooted in the feeling that his or her feelings and thoughts are valuable and important to a parent, to the family, and to his or her community of friends and schoolmates.

"What do you think?"

"What's your idea?"

These are questions adults take for granted as common fare in our relationships, especially in our workplace or in daily conversation with spouses and friends. But how uncommon these questions often are in relationships between adults and children! Not that children don't have thoughts, opinions, or ideas to express. It's just that adults rarely ask. Perhaps even worse, adults often cut short a child's attempts to convey ideas and feelings.

Do you really know your child's opinion? Do you know what he or she is thinking, or imagining? Have you asked lately?

Even at very early ages, children begin to form opinions, largely in the form of likes and dislikes. They respond favorably to some things, reject others. As they experience their world, some events stand out, others don't. They have ideas about the way things ought to be. Often, their ideas are rooted in fantasy rather than reality. Still, they've got an idea and from their perspective, it's a worthy idea.

Boosting a feeling of self-value in a child can be done simply when an adult, especially a parent, turns to a child in the middle of a conversation, and says, "And what about you? What do you think? How do you feel about this? Do you have any ideas?"

Include your child in dinner time conversation. Take time to hear out his or her ideas.

Don't criticize your child's opinions. As opinions, they are as valid as anyone's. Let your child know that whatever his or her opinion, it's OK to express it.

Don't make fun of your child's ideas. Don't hack away at your child's lack of logic or the "unworkableness" of your child's ideas. The process of telling and exploring ideas is, after all, the way your child comes to form ideas and, eventually, to come up with better ideas. Ask your child, "What do you think would happen if we did that?" Or, "Do you think this would work all the time, or just in this particular case?" You may be surprised at the creative twists and turns such a conversation can take!

Don't totally discount the validity of your child's opinion, even if it's ill-founded. Avoid declaring with a tone of finality, "That's rubbish." Instead, say to your child, "I'll consider that," or "I'll take that under advisement." In nearly all cases, a child isn't nearly as concerned that an idea be enacted as he or she is delighted that the idea has been expressed.

The most important result of establishing conversation between adult and child is that a child might remain willing to express his or her thoughts and feelings throughout life. A child who is rarely or never asked for an idea or an opinion is highly unlikely to emerge as a teenager willing to talk freely with a parent about drugs, sex, God, or life goals! A child whose ideas and feelings are never explored or appreciated is unlikely to become an adult who freely expresses opinions to parents.

The child with high self-esteem and confidence is a child who can look in the mirror and say, "My ideas have merit. My opinions have validity. My thoughts are worth expressing." All of these statements are translated within the spirit of the child as: "I have value." And *that* feeling is at the very heart of self-esteem!

9 ■ Have a Gallery for Your Child's Work

One of the easiest and most effective ways of letting children know we value them is to value the work they produce or create. One of the easiest and most effective ways of doing that is by displaying the work in a prominent place.

For some the display area is the refrigerator door. For others it's a bulletin board in the kitchen or family room. Or it may be a frame on the wall (in which artwork can be quickly and easily placed) or clipboard hanging on the side of a cabinet.

Displaying your child's work is a clear signal that the work is regarded as important, valid, and appreciated. Let's explore each of those concepts briefly.

Show that you believe the work is important. When you display your child's work you are giving it importance. Your child sees you throw away junk mail, discard the daily paper, and toss out extraneous instructions and advertisements. In fact, your child sees you throw away more paper than you ever keep! The message to your child is that there's a lot of paper that Mom and Dad simply don't want.

When you keep your child's work and display it your

child gets a different message: His or her work counts. Because the child's work is often a direct expression of self, the message is that the *child* is important. If the work is wanted, he or she is wanted, too.

Show that your child's work is valid. Much of your child's artwork isn't going to make any sense to you. It may not look pretty. You may not even know what it is your child is depicting or expressing! But, by keeping and displaying your child's creations, you are doing two things. First, you are acknowledging his or her artwork as a valid aesthetic expression. And in that, you are encouraging your child to continue to express thoughts, feelings, and imagination openly. You are saying, "So this is how you see the world. That's neat. That's your perspective. I like seeing how you view the world."

Second, you are inviting your child to continue to express his or her personality, character, and talents in other ways. The child may think, *"Hmmm, if Mom or Dad thinks this artwork is cool, well, I'll do a dance, or write a poem, or paint another picture."*

Show that your child's work is appreciated. Your child's creative expressions are your child's gifts to you, freely given, most of the time. Be a good receiver of these gifts.

If your child is giving you a test or paper with a good grade on it, your child is saying to you, "See what I did." Such a paper isn't a gift as much as it's an award shared. Express your appreciation for the effort, skill, and study that your child put into earning that good mark.

If your child is giving you artwork, accept it as a gift of art shared not only with you but with the world at large. Find something in the artwork about which you can comment honestly. "I sure like the colors you used." "I like the way you used such bold strokes."

How long should you keep your child's accomplishments and expressions up for view? That will depend, in part, on how productive your child is.

You may simply exchange one set of school papers for another. You may want to keep several pictures on display simultaneously. Whatever you decide, don't let your child see you throw the old work away. Simply discard it discreetly.

A word of caution: never post something about which your child expresses embarrassment or dislike. Even though you may think the picture is "cute," your child may regard it as less than a good effort. Go with your child's evaluation.

Having a gallery for your child's work is a way of saying to the world, "A child lives here. That child is pretty special. In fact, here's proof of just how special that child is to all of us." That's a self-esteem building message of the first order!

10 ■ Help Your Child Make Friends

Children don't automatically know how to make friends. In fact, as rather self-centered beings with a strong "mine!" orientation, they usually find that making friends can be tough work!

Because your child may know he or she is a valued and loved member of the family, your child may expect that the rest of the world automatically feels the same way. Your child is likely to go into the "big world" and expect others to come when called, give when asked, and smile even when the child is grouchy.

Your child may have very little experience with others the same age. He or she may be used to "bigger" kids, assuming something of a subservient role, or being the "baby," a station that carries with it a certain amount of power. Encountering children the same age—especially a large group—is a new experience.

What can you do to help children make friends?

Enter into play with your child and the "new friend." You don't need to stay long and shouldn't. But at the outset of a new relationship, it's a good idea to enter into the play for a while. Most parents don't realize that children need to be taught how to play with things and with one another.

Teach your child some ice-breaker phrases, such as, "Hi, my name's _____. *What's yours?"* That's perhaps the most common line of self-introduction of all time, but it works. Share with your child some of the questions you've come to regard as second nature. "Where are you from?" "What games do you like to play?"

Give your child ample freedom to invite friends to your home. Granted, you don't need to operate Grand Central Station, but you can establish certain hours and days, as well as limits to the number of children allowed at your house at any one time.

Recognize that children go through "ups and downs" with their friends the same way adults experience estrangements, distance, and closeness with their friends. Don't expect your child's friendships to run smoothly. They won't.

Encourage your child to have many friends. The child who is limited to just one "best friend" is likely to experience a major heartache or disappointment should that friend move away or become estranged.

Don't expect your child to like every person you like. Parents often identify the "ideal friend" for their child; rarely does the child share that opinion. Let your child's friendships be forged by your child, not by you.

Making and keeping friends is a major life-skill. It requires communication, patience, and a willingness to share experiences.

11 ■ The Importance of Feeling Important

Self-esteem is based on value—specifically, the way in which children value themselves.

Every child has an inherent sense of self. It's in a social context, however, that the child comes to place self along a "value" scale. Children aren't born with either high or low self-esteem.

A child learns that he or she has value in two ways. First, someone that the child admires, loves, and respects tells the child that he or she is special and valuable. Second, in the course of appraising his or her own contributions to family, friends, and the larger community the child recognizes his or her worth.

Let's explore these avenues leading toward the building of self-esteem a little bit more.

A child must hear approval and encouragement from an adult he or she admires, loves, and respects. Here are some statements of approval your child needs to hear from you:

- "God must certainly have loved us to have given us you for a son."
- "Nobody can take your place."

- "You are valuable beyond measure."
- "Nobody on this earth can fill the place I have for you in my heart."

These are all affirmations of who a child is—not words or praise for what a child does.

There's a difference between words of approval for the child and words of approval for the child's deeds. It's like separating the sin from the sinner. You may punish or discipline a child for what he or she does, but punishment should focus upon deeds.

I can't think of anything sadder, or more destructive to a child, than for a parent to say in a fit of rage, "You're worthless. You're no good. You're a mistake. I wish you were out of my life." And yet, many parents silently convey that message by failing to separate deed from child when they execute punishment or convey their disappointment in a child's behavior.

It's a wise parent who says, "Joanne, I'm grounding you for the weekend because you have failed to do what I asked you to do. I want you to learn to follow instructions because I love you and want you to have a successful life. You're going to have to be dependable to an employer someday. You're going to have to be able to follow instructions and to be on time. You're important enough to me to punish you now, because of who I know you are and will be in the future."

Your child's self-esteem will ultimately be defined by your child. Eventually, your child needs to reach the point where he or she says: "I'm somebody to be admired, loved, and respected! I admire, love, and respect myself."

You can help your child build self-esteem by

- pointing out to your child instances in which he or she has been honest and fair. "I'm glad you're an honest person, Joey. No one should be more highly regarded than an honest person."
- acknowledging the "giving" acts of your child. "Sharing your toys was a very loving thing for you to do, Tim."
- applauding the way in which your child shows responsibility. "I'm very pleased, Jon, that I hardly ever need to remind you to feed your cat. You're becoming a very responsible young man."

A child who hears comments such as these eventually will appraise his or her actions and note, "I'm doing the right thing in this situation. If I don't do it, no one will. I'm valuable."

Or, the child will note, "I'm giving of myself and possessions and that's good. If I don't give, this person might not ever receive gifts or compassion from anyone. I have a valuable role to fill."

Or, the child will note, "I'm showing responsibility. If I don't take responsibility, perhaps no one will. I'm going to see that this job is done and done right."

Value connected to self. That's self-esteem.

12 ■ Pray with and for Your Child

Your child needs to know that he or she is not only important to you but important to God as well. Let your child know he or she has value for all eternity!

At an early age children can grasp the concept of a God who will listen to them at all times. What a comfort that knowledge is to a child who has a parent who travels a great deal, often works late, or may not be around owing to divorce, separation, or death.

There's no substitute for saying to your child, and saying it often, "God loves you. I do, too."

One father I know tells his son regularly, "God created you. And God doesn't make junk."

One mother I know sings her favorite song to her children at least once a week—not because she schedules it, but because she loves the song and is quick to share it: "His eye is on the sparrow, and I know He watches you." It's no wonder that her children know all the verses to that hymn and are sometimes overheard singing them quietly to themselves!

Perhaps the most encouraging way to convey to children that they are important to God is to pray regularly with them, and for them.

What a comfort for a child to be pulled up on the lap of a mother and held close as she prays:

"Heavenly Father, I'm so grateful that You created Liz and sent her to be a part of our family. I'm so grateful that You gave her a quick smile, a big dose of creativity, and lots of energy and health. I know how much You love her and that You only want good things for her. Help me to be a good mother to Liz. Help Liz to grow up to be a woman who loves You all the days of her life."

What a self-esteem boost for a little boy to have his father kneel by his bed and pray:

"Heavenly Father, thank You for giving us Kurt. Help me to be a good father to him. Help him to grow up strong and healthy. Help him always to be willing to do his best and give his best."

Assure your child that you believe God hears and answers prayers. Assure your child that God's answers are always based on love for your child.

A child who grows up believing she or he is important to God—and valued and loved by Him—is a child who isn't afraid of the future. He's got an eternal ally on his side. She's got a sense of worth that transcends the present. He's confident that no matter what he faces, a higher authority and a greater power than even Mom or Dad is on his side.

13 ■ The Importance of Good Language Skills

Early in life, your child will have a keen awareness of whether he or she is "fitting in" with peers, schoolmates, or teammates. The ability to fit in is important. It helps give the child self-definition. It helps the child form a sense of what role to play in a group and a sense of belonging and acceptance.

A number of factors will be subconsciously monitored by your child and others to determine whether he or she "fits." Perhaps the common denominator of these factors—over which you have some control and ability to train—is language. It's critically important that your child be able to speak the same language as those around him or her.

If your child speaks a language other than English and lives in an English-speaking nation, make certain your child learns English, too, at a very early age. The same holds true for an English-speaking child living among non-English speakers. Don't let your child be linguistically handicapped in the larger society.

Language skills also include the ability to be fluent and readily understood in the common language of the culture, and to speak without "impediments" that might cause others to misunderstand.

Your child will need speech therapy. At some point in their development, most children need corrective therapy, even if its only that provided by a mom or dad who says, "Say it this way. . . ." If your child has problems lasting longer than a couple of months, have his or her hearing checked. If there are no hearing problems, arrange for professional help if the speech impediment doesn't clear up after six months. Most schools have speech therapy programs in elementary grades. Your pediatrician is also a good resource for recommending speech teachers. The earlier the coping, remediating, or compensating skills are learned, the better the results.

Don't assume that your child will simply grow out of a speech problem. That may not happen. Furthermore, your child may be socially ostracized or stigmatized in the meantime. Again, fitting in among peers is important. Don't let a speech impediment stand in the way if it can be corrected.

Your child will need grammar therapy. I've yet to meet a child that has never made a grammatical error. Making mistakes are part of learning language. Children will try out various combinations of words; if incorrect combinations aren't corrected, the child is left with the impression that he or she has spoken correctly, and the child will likely adopt the wrong pattern of words.

When you hear grammatical mistakes, gently correct them. Be consistent and persistent.

Good grammar is a calling card for your child, not only at school, but throughout life. Many people have been overlooked for promotions because of bad grammar (although that may not be the stated reason). Many children have been judged intellectually inferior or of a "lower class" because of bad grammar. Don't let your child grow up with the handicap of bad grammar. It may well keep him or her from fitting in later in life.

Your child's language will need editing. Children learn words from peers and television that parents don't want as part of the child's vocabulary. Children find pleasure in trying out the sound of certain words. Some of those words are going to be curse words. Some will be slang phrases. Some will be derogatory or racist remarks. It's a parent's responsibility to say, "We don't say that." Or, "That's not a word we use." Otherwise, the child will assume that the word is an acceptable one.

A child with good language skills has confidence that he or she can communicate in a socially acceptable manner. He or she has the assurance of fitting in.

Good language skills do not automatically build self-esteem, but bad language habits can bring about the rejection and criticism that destroys self-esteem. Don't let that happen to your child.

14 ■ Teach Your Child How to Read and Follow Written Instructions

A big part of your child's sense of self-confidence comes from the ability to know what to do in emergency situations, when solving problems, and when trying to get things done.

How do you teach your child what to do? First, you admit to yourself that you can't teach your child every response to every possible situation or circumstance. Your responsibility is to teach your child how to get answers and how to discover what needs to be done.

One of the best ways I know to help a child feel confident in facing the unknown is to train the child to look for, use, and follow instruction manuals.

For some time, a little card was taped to our refrigerator door. It read, "If at first you don't succeed, try reading the instructions."

The discouraging fact is that most of us don't turn to the instruction manual at the outset of a project or when something goes wrong. We fumble around until the item is mostly put together (except for that one odd screw) or mostly repaired (except for the occasional spark).

The encouraging fact is that upwards of ninety percent of the nitty-gritty, everyday fix-it problems we face in life can be overcome by consulting the right instruction booklet or owner's manual.

Instruction manuals and how-to books are readily available to tell you how to build, repair, or improve nearly every area of your life—from furniture scratches to carburetors.

The two key questions your child needs to consider are: "What do you need to know?" And, "Where can you find an instruction booklet?"

The most effective way for your child to learn to consider these questions is to hear you ask them of yourself and watch you consult instruction booklets.

Invite your child to help you put things together, repair things, or solve a problem. Show how instruction booklets are laid out and how to relate diagrams and pictures to real objects. Point out the importance of doing step 1 before step 2. Ask, "What would you do next?" Or, "Read me the next step, will you?" Let the child have hands-on experience in putting together the new baby crib or the toy train set. Encourage the child to consult instructions before loading batteries into the new tape recorder.

Encourage your children to make things on their own

that require consulting a set of instructions. For example:

- making a cake requires a recipe (actually a set of instructions)
- sewing a dress requires a pattern (including a set of instructions)
- building a model airplane requires a step-by-step set of instructions

The child that grows up reading instructions and helping to put together, repair, or build things has two great advantages in life. First, he or she believes that most broken things *can* be fixed. That's an excellent orientation to have, especially as it may relate later in life to health, marriage, or interpersonal conflicts. Second, the child believes there are logical, specific steps to most processes. The child will learn not to expect "abracadabra" miracles.

Self-confidence is enhanced when your child knows he or she is capable of repairing or improving a broken object or difficult situation. Learning to read and follow instructions provides your child with the ability to do just that.

15 ■ Set Rules

Parents have the authority to make rules that children are required to follow. Parents also have the responsibility to make rules that will benefit a child.

Authority and responsibility go hand in hand. As long as you are responsible (legally, spiritually, financially, physically, morally) for your child, you have parental authority. In other words, as long as you are paying your child's way in life, you have the authority to make sure your child takes care of possessions and limits purchases to things that meet your approval. As long as you have legal responsibility for your child, you have the authority to make certain that he or she obeys the law and respects all those in leadership.

Children crave rules, although they may never admit it in so many words. Why? Because rules provide both freedom and security.

Rules provide freedom? Yes, they establish boundaries in which freedom can reign. Consider the parent who says, "You may ride your bike up to the end of the sidewalk. You may not go into the street or ride on the lawns." Or, "You may play any place you want to in the backyard." Those are options a child can embrace and in which a child can create, explore, and move without fear.

Rules also help establish a world of known behaviors and their consequences. "Leave the backyard, and you will face punishment."

Rules help establish a world in which it's safe to try out new things. "You can make anything you want with this clay, but you must keep the clay on the table."

Rules help establish the boundaries of a relationship. "You may not speak to your mother in that tone of voice."

Rules help establish the limits of a parent's expectations. "You must make your bed" carries with it the unspoken implication that the child is *not* expected to make all the beds or clean the entire house.

Make certain that a child knows the rules by which the family is to operate. Describe your expectations, establish the boundaries, and state and restate rules as often as necessary.

Make certain that you are consistent, persistent, and fair about rules. That means establishing appropriate and fair punishments for broken rules. That means punishing a child each time the rule is broken willfully.

Let children know why you are punishing them. Restate the rule. Better yet, ask children to tell you why they think they are being punished.

A child who has the security of rules, which are consistently and persistently applied, knows that Mom and Dad care enough to restrain, constrain, and train.

16 ■ Teach Your Child Basic First-Aid Skills

Self-confidence is believing you know what to do in a given situation. At no time is self-confidence more necessary than in a medical emergency.

Your children or your entire family can enroll in a first-aid and CPR course. The Red Cross, or perhaps your local YWCA or YMCA, offer such courses periodically. Local adult education programs might also provide first-aid training. At the very least, parents should take such a course and have an up-to-date first-aid manual handy so that they can pass on accurate information and basic skills to their children.

Teach your children how to dial "911" in case of emergencies. Rehearse the number with them often. Show them how to dial and how to speak clearly into the phone. (Of course, your children must be able to give their name and address. Teach that information first!) Practice these skills periodically until you are certain your children know exactly what to do in a crisis.

Have a periodic fire drill with your child. Show him or her how to get down on hands and knees and find the nearest escape route out of the house. Warn your child never to return to a burning building, no matter the reason.

Teach your children early what this symbol means:

Tell them not to even think about touching, tasting, or using anything having that symbol.

Encourage your child to come and tell you if anything is amiss that might cause someone harm, for example, an electric socket left uncapped, a gun, or a pill container out of the medicine cabinet.

"Don't touch, run, and tell" is a good sequence of actions to teach, and it can be learned from age two.

Giving your child first-aid and accident-prevention skills says to your child, "I love you enough to want you to stay alive! I value your safety and health—indeed, your very life." That adds to a child's sense of worth and self-esteem.

First-aid and accident-prevention skills also give your child confidence that he or she has the capability to act in emergency situations. That confidence will not only benefit your child, but any person experiencing an emergency in your child's presence!

17 ■ Answer Your Child's Questions

Encourage your child to ask questions. Such encouragement says to your child, "I want you to know. I want you to grow." When your child asks, answer. Your child will think, *Mom and Dad consider me valuable enough to teach and train.* In perceived value lies self-esteem.

You will not have answers for all of your child's questions. Admit that openly. Don't let your child grow up believing you know everything and can solve every problem without assistance.

If you don't have an answer, explore ways in which you might find an answer. Have a map or globe available for ready consultation. Invest in reference books written for children.

I recently encountered a low-income family that didn't have money for such tools. However, they kept a running list of questions. Once a week, the mother would gather her children together for a visit to their local library, where they would explore answers together, often with the aid of a librarian.

Answer your child's questions as honestly as you can. "I don't know" can be an honest answer to a "why, how, when, where, or who" question. However, some parents use "I don't know" as a means of ending a conversation. Don't fall into that trap. Simply say, "Honey, I'm trying to concentrate on something else right now. Ask me that question at another time, OK?"

Answer your child's questions as completely as possible. Give your child as much information as your child *needs* to know. Feel free to ask your child, "What brings this question to your mind?" Try to get a context for your child's question before providing an answer.

Don't tell your child more details than he or she needs to know. On the other hand, to give your child a "pat" or "easy" answer to a complex problem is also a disservice.

Always answer a question in a way that will benefit your child. "Why are you divorcing each other?" asks your four-year-old. "Because Mommy and Daddy can't figure out how to live together right now. We both love you very much, but we are having a problem communicating with each other, and we're angry all the time. That is making us sick. So we're separating right now. We both want to be with you and spend time with you. We both love you no matter what happens between us." Such an answer benefits the child.

Children learn by asking questions and receiving answers. They not only learn facts and principles. They learn that you are willing to field questions and that you give value to their inquiries. To give value to a child's questions is to impart value to the child.

18 ■ Keep Your Promises

What happens when a promise made by an adult to a child is kept? The child intuitively knows the adult has told the truth.

A child cannot always grasp that a kept promise has meant a sacrifice of time and money, or an exertion of effort and ability. A child may not be familiar with the concepts of cost, time, or obligation.

A child's self-esteem and confidence are ultimately only as good as the "truth" he or she perceives in the world. The child needs facts, solid answers, a truthful description of an adult's feelings, and fixed boundaries for his or her behavior. The child needs to be able to differentiate between lie and truth, if he or she is ever to differentiate among a long list of possibilities, or know the difference between reality and fantasy. To identify that which is true and real, a child needs valid, concrete evidence.

A kept promise is an incident of truth to a child. The kept promise says, "Daddy said this, and he did it. What he says to me is true." Or, "Mommy promised me we would go, and we went. I can trust Mommy to tell me other things, and they will be true too."

A kept promise is also a great act of love and care.
That's because the thing promised to a child is almost
always perceived as a good gift. "I promise you we'll go
to the park on Saturday," says a parent. Going to the
park together is a gift of time and love. A child may not
be able to define it in those terms, but he or she feels it
in that way. Things promised are generally "good
things." They are presents.

A kept promise says to a child, "I value our relationship. I love you enough to make the effort to do what
I've told you I'm going to do."

What about the unkept promise?

An unkept promise is perceived by the child as an
example of lie-telling. It's perceived as an example of
love withheld.

"But what about those times when I just can't follow
through on a promise?" you ask.

Tell your child that you are sorry you've disappointed him or her. Don't make up an excuse. Don't
discount the importance of the promise. Ask your child,
sincerely, to forgive you for not keeping your promise.

A child will understand and forgive the occasional
unkept promise. A pattern of broken promises, however, is not so easily forgiven or forgotten.

Promises are best limited to the concrete realm,
places you'll go, things you'll do, items you'll buy, or
events you'll experience. A child can readily understand, anticipate, and appreciate such promises when
kept.

Don't promise your child changes in your own behavior, such as, "Baby, I promise you I'm going to stop drinking." Or, "Darling, I promise you I'll never lie to you again." There's too big a chance you won't be able to keep such a promise. Don't compound your lack of good behavior or self-control with what your child will perceive to be a lie and an act of love withheld.

The best rule for promises: If you don't intend to make a one-hundred percent effort to keep a promise, don't make it. It's better not to make any promises than to make them and break them. Corollary rule: If you've already made a promise and see that you aren't going to be able to keep it, admit it early. If at all possible provide an alternative.

Kept promises put a child on sure ground. The child grows with an understanding of what and whom can be trusted. Your child's estimation of his or her own value goes up. Unkept promises whittle away at a child's self-esteem and self-confidence.

If you are going to err, err on the side of making too few promises and keeping them, than making too many promises and failing to follow through.

19 ■ Teach Your Child Basic Cooking Skills

What is the one skill that will be useful—even necessary—to your child all of his or her life? Not the ability to throw a touchdown pass. Not the ability to score a perfect grade on a math test. Not the ability to match accessories to a dress. No, it's the ability to prepare food!

Knowing simple cooking skills can build a child's confidence, and assure the child that he or she can handle a degree of independence.

What does a child need to know?

In this day and age, cooking techniques can be rather simple. A child needs to

- know how to open a can and heat its contents in a pan on a stove.
- learn to boil eggs, cook boil-in-the-bag meals, and prepare frozen vegetables.
- know how to microwave a prepared meal.
- know how to measure with measuring cups and spoons, how to read a recipe.
- know how to turn on an oven (and set its temperature), how to turn on range-top burners, and how to avoid getting burned.

- know how to operate a mixer, a toaster, and a blender.
- know how to choose fruits, vegetables, and meats for quality and freshness.
- know how to wash dishes, set a table, and scrub and peel fruits and vegetables.

Most of these things your child will learn easily and quickly, if you will let your child watch you and work with you as you shop and prepare meals.

Be willing to let your child make a mess, break an egg or two, and get a little flour on the kitchen floor.

Begin by giving your child simple things to do. Then give your child more and more to do as he or she becomes adept with kitchen tools. Encourage your teen to have a "famous recipe" or two that are all his or her own. One man I know taught his son what he considered to be the three essentials of domestic life: how to wash his clothes, how to iron a shirt, and how to make chili! Give your teenager the satisfaction of preparing an entire meal from time to time.

Even a very young child can help set the table, clear dishes, and scrub vegetables with a vegetable brush.

Again, self-confidence is rooted in a child's perception that he or she has abilities and is capable of responding adequately in a given situation. Give your child confidence in the kitchen. Give your children the assurance that they'll be able to fix a meal for themselves.

20 ■ The Strength of Blessing

A major step in your child's development of self-esteem will come when your child is able to spontaneously and generously compliment, "bless" or show appreciation for another person.

That kind of behavior from your child, perhaps more than any other kind of behavior, says to the world, "I have value. I'm not afraid that by complimenting, applauding, or appreciating someone else I will diminish my own worth."

The child who knows his or her value can not be deflated is the child who can give attention to another child or share the limelight. The child who knows he or she cannot lose personal value is the one who has the inner strength and power to "bless" others.

You cannot dictate that kind of spontaneous behavior from your child. You can watch for it and applaud it when it happens, however. And, you can help prepare in your child the willingness to respond with praise and compliments for others.

Encourage your child to tell you about some of the good things that others do or say. I recently overheard Dixie talking with her son Blake. "You made a great play in scoring that goal. What do you think were the other outstanding plays of the game?"

Notice that Dixie opened her question with a compliment to her own son. She modeled the behavior she hoped her son would adopt.

Blake responded, "Well, Kerry made a great save when he blocked a goal attempt."

"What did you think of that long pass that Tad made?"

"That's what set me up! Sam stole the ball, Tad got it, shot it over to me, and wham—into the net!"

Dixie continued, "Next time we see Tad's mother, let's tell her you think he did a great job. We don't need to make a big deal of it. You could say something like, 'I'm sure glad Tad is on my team. He's a great passer.' That will mean a lot to Tad's mother."

Notice that Dixie gave Blake something specific to say. She didn't require that he generate the compliment. Another good move!

When Dixie and Blake saw Tad's mother a few days later, Blake spoke up. "I'm sure glad Tad's on my team. He's a great passer!"

Tad's mother said, "Why, thank you, Blake. I'll tell Tad. That will mean a lot coming from you, since you're the team's top scorer." Blake beamed.

It won't be long before Blake will be confident enough to say directly to Tad after a game (perhaps even in front of the entire team). "Great pass, Tad. You really set up that point."

Avoid linking rewards or future behavior with compli-

ments. Don't promise to reward your child for complimenting someone. In other words, don't say, "Go up
and tell Jennie what a good job she did, and then I'll
take you out for ice cream." Don't link compliments
with manipulation. Don't say, "Tell Daddy what a good
job he did making dinner, and maybe he'll let you go
with him bowling after supper." Let compliments stand
for what they are—an act of giving praise and approval
from one human being to another.

Value, don't devalue, compliments. Many people don't
know how to receive a compliment gracefully. Don't let
your child say, "Oh, it was nothing." Teach your child
how to say, "Thank you. I'm glad you liked it." Or,
"Thank you. It makes me feel good to hear that."

Finally, *encourage your child to compliment others by
being free with your own compliments of other adults.*
Model the behavior you want your child to copy. Be
generous in applauding others, in calling attention to
their successes, and in appreciating their contributions.

If you show that you value your child, he or she will
learn to value himself. Teach your child that a sense of
self-worth will be strengthened, not diminished, when
he or she compliments and shows appreciation to others.

21 ■ Give Your Child a Teamwork Experience

Encourage your child to be part of a team. In fact, through the course of his or her childhood, your child can benefit from being part of several teams.

Your child could play team sports. Soccer, especially, is a good sport for young boys and girls. Softball is also good for younger children. Basketball requires a fairly high skill level and is probably best for older children and teens. (I suggest you avoid football as long as your child is still growing; the risk of injuries to connective tissues is high.)

Tennis, golf, swimming, track and field, and gymnastics teams provide opportunities for individual competition, and at the same time, provide team morale and identity. Or your choice might be a competitive team in a nonphysical arena, such as a chess team.

What does team involvement provide for your child?

As part of a team, your child is exposed to a coach other than yourself. Your child learns to take instructions and to receive encouragement from an adult who is neither parent or teacher.

As part of a team, your child is exposed to an activity that is highly goal focused. Most school and family activities do not have clear-cut short-term goals. In competitive events, of course, the goal is to win. In non-competitive teams, the goal is generally to perform successfully.

As part of a team, your child will be exposed to the concept of morale. Your child will learn valuable lessons in how to build morale, how to forge and maintain a group identity, and how to lose gracefully without getting irretrievably "down."

As part of a team, your child will learn that his or her own performance can vary from day to day, and that losing a game rarely means losing an entire season. Your child will learn that most team events are the composite of individual roles, individual abilities, and individual efforts. These are good lessons that extend into adulthood.

Group competition generally provides broader and more favorable experiences than does individual competition. Wins and losses are shared when the victory or defeat is the result of team play. The long-term value of competition for a child is probably keyed more to the experience of loss than to winning. Knowing how to lose gracefully is one of the greatest lessons your child can ever learn.

Many other group activities that require team effort are available to your child beyond those that provide competition. Bands, orchestras, and choirs are teams, of sorts. They require group effort and coordination of individual activities toward common goals.

Campfire, Boy Scouts, Girl Scouts, Royal Rangers,

and other children's associations also provide many of the advantages of team involvement.

How should you go about choosing which activity is right for your child?

Talk to your child about it, and let your child have a say in the decision. If your child hates softball and loves playing the trumpet, opt for summer band opportunities over Little League.

Another important factor for you to consider is the coach. Is this a person you trust with your child? Is the coach a person who demands perfection or gets angry easily? A good coach teaches the principle rules of the game and stands up for fairness and teamwork.

What if your child wants to quit?

Find out why. In most cases, children enjoy being part of a team. When a child wants to quit a team, it usually has nothing to do with the pleasure he or she gets from playing the game. Often children want to quit because of pressures from parents, coach, or themselves to perform well.

Teams also provide a child an identity beyond his family. They provide a role for your child to fill other than that of "middle daughter" or "youngest son." The child who is a valued member of a team—whether it be as a second baseman, a bass drum player, or one of the tenors—sees himself or herself as a more valuable person *in toto*. And that's self-esteem!

22 ■ Encourage Your Child to Ask Questions

The most efficient way for your child to gain information and to improve academic performance is by asking the right questions to get the answers he or she needs.

Asking questions takes courage, positive self-esteem, and self-confidence. Stated another way, the greater your child's self-esteem and confidence levels, the more likely your child will ask questions.

Most children start out asking questions. "Why?" seems to be the all-time favorite question of children. Unfortunately, this question is often asked as a challenge to authority, not truly as a quest for information. Parents know that. The sad result is that many parents lose patience with their "why babies" and squelch the entire questioning process in the course of exerting their authority.

Parents need to differentiate between the true question and the challenge to authority. Be generous in giving your timing, attention, and care to those questions that are truly aimed at getting information.

How do you encourage the right kinds of questions? *Ask* those kinds of questions!

Ask your child questions as you consult maps together—even if it's only the map of stores in the mall. "Which way do you suppose is the shortest way to that store?" Ask your child questions as you ride bikes together. "How many miles do you think we have gone?"

One of my favorite approaches to asking questions of older children and teens is to ask them to pretend to be an inventor, builder, or creator. For example: "Look at that new house, Cory. What kinds of questions do you suppose the builder had to ask before he could build that house?"

Children's questions tend to force a parent to be specific, concrete, or to admit they don't know everything. Those are painful moments for many parents. "Why are there so many stars?" is a tough question. Do your best, but admit it when you don't know the answer to a question.

The more your child asks questions and gets good answers, the more your child will feel confident in asking questions. That confidence could save your child's life someday: "What's the fastest way to the hospital?" It could help your child make a major scientific discovery someday. "What happens when we add this element to that mixture?"

Teach your child to ask questions. That says to your child, "I want you to know. I value you enough to want you to be an intelligent, inquisitive, exploring adult. I value your right to know, and I value your desire to know."

23 ■ The Star

Every child has the capacity to win at something. Your challenge as a parent is to find that something!

Assume that your child may not be good at the things you are good at. My father has outstanding mechanical ability. He can take apart, fix, and put back together virtually anything. My brother and I are far better at breaking things than fixing them. Dad can't understand why we can't fix things; we can't understand how he does!

Assume, too, that your child may not like the things you like. Larry likes to play golf. His son thinks it's the stupidest game he's ever been around. These differences are not merely a matter of children rebelling against parents for the sake of exerting their own identity. People are simply different.

Finally, assume your child may not have the career you want him or her to have. You are better off assuming that your child is *not* going to be a doctor, lawyer, millionaire, president of the nation, or the inheritor of your business.

Parents are better advised to help children succeed at their choice of careers, than to make everyone's life miserable trying to dictate their child's future! A son or daughter who is miserable, angry, or bitter at his or her choice of job, profession, or vocation is not likely to be a success at it. Let your child choose personal goals and walk his or her own path.

How do you find the "star" in your child?

Watch what your child likes to do. Where is your child's interest? What makes your child truly excited? As long as it's moral and legal, encourage that activity!

Stuart loved to watch airplanes. He could hardly be torn away from the airport when the family went to pick up visiting relatives. He bought airplane posters, books about airplanes, and even instructions for making a light-wing, single-engine, single-passenger aircraft. His mother had a phobia about flying and hated the thought of her son in a plane. Still, she could see this wasn't an interest that would wane. So, she bought Stuart model airplane kits. She allowed him to get a part-time job and use his earnings for flying lessons. Today, Stuart is a commercial pilot. His mother still takes the train, but she knows her son is in the "dream" job he always desired.

To help your child become a "star," you must first help your child find the right stage on which he or she can perform his or her best and brightest number.

Once you've located that interest, do your best to help your child develop the fullest potential of his or her abilities. If your child is interested in theater, take your child to plays, and get backstage to talk with actors and stage managers, if at all possible. Give your child the opportunity to be a part of children's theater programs. Attend your child's school plays. Your child may one day paint sets for the local community theater rather than star on the big screen, but he or she will still be a star on his or her own stage.

But what about that day when the child's interests change?

That often happens. In fact, expect it. Rarely do people know all their lives what they want to pursue as a career.

Whatever changes in interest may occur, don't count the experiences you've provided your child as losses. Count them as enrichment. Count them as opportunities you gave your child to explore his or her talents, to develop certain skills, and to grow in self-discipline through practice and practical experience.

And finally, have reasonable expectations of your child. On any sports field, in any recital, on any test, there's only one "best." Your child may not be *the* star. That doesn't mean she can't be *a* star.

A child who learns to overcome stage fright, to master a new skill, or to learn a new part is a child who grows in confidence. A child who learns to overcome failure through discipline, practice, and more practice is a child who comes to value his or her own strength of character.

Give your child the opportunity to walk onto a chosen "stage," to do his or her best, and to hear your "Bravo!"

24 ■ Give a Reason for Your Decisions Whenever Possible

Whenever possible, give your child a reason for the things you ask him or her to do or not to do. This says to your child, "I have thought this through. I value your life too much to treat you in a willy-nilly way. I count you worthy of an explanation."

Granted, there are many times in life when providing a reason is impractical. This is especially true when it comes to *commands*. Your child needs to learn to heed your commands without question. "Run!" should mean run. You don't want your child standing in the path of a runaway car while waiting for you to give an explanation!

Explain in a general way the reason for your commands. Let your child know that when you say, "Run!" "Stop!" "Don't!" "Move!" you expect immediate and prompt obedience, generally because pain, harm, or damage is imminent.

Requests, however, differ from commands. Requests are things you ask your child to do because you prefer or need those things to be done. "I'd like for you to rake the lawn today" is a request. Your child's life isn't in danger. "It's time for you to set the table." Although it may sound like a command to your child, that, too, is really a request.

What rationale can be provided for simple requests?

"Because you're a part of this family and each person in a family has to do things to help the family. As a parent, I get to ask you to do certain things. That's my job." That's reason enough for reasonable requests.

There are other requests, however, that are going to seem out-of-the-norm to your child. Those are the ones you need to explain. "Starting on Monday, Joan, you're going to be riding the bus to school." Such a new routine in a child's life deserves an explanation. "I'm starting a new part-time job at the hospital next week, and I need to leave the house when you do. I won't have time to drive you to school first. I'll be here until you get on the bus each morning, and I'll be here when you get off in the afternoon. Today, we're going to go to the school to see where the bus drops you off and where you will get on it in the afternoon."

There may be times when you feel hard-pressed to come up with a good reason. You always have the prerogative as a parent to say, "Hmmm. My parental instincts tell me 'no.' And since I'm the parent, I have to go with my parental instincts. I may be wrong. But my instincts are all I have to go on, so you'll just have to trust me this time." Most decisions are made based on the way a person feels, not on logic!

Avoid basing your reasons on "absolutes." For example, there's no magic age when children should start to date. Saying to your child, "You can't date until you can drive" gives you little room for evaluating your son or daughter's development as a teen. Perhaps your teenager won't be mature enough to date even when sixteen! On the other hand, perhaps a double date to a school dance will seem appropriate when your teen is fourteen. Don't box yourself in. This principle carries over to issues such as wearing make-up, shaving legs, piercing ears, going alone to movies, or staying overnight at a friend's house. Don't take the easy way out by establishing "magic ages."

Evaluate your child as an individual. Move with your child at his or her own developmental rate. Trust your child as he or she grows in trustworthiness. Loosen the parental ties according to your child's level of maturity. That approach says to your child, "I value you as you, not as an 'average child' or a 'statistic' or as 'everybody else.' I will make decisions for you and explain them to you in a way I think is right for you, not for every other kid on the block. You're a distinct individual. I care about all of your life, not just this one particular moment."

A child who hears reasons for requests and directives will grow to believe he or she is a person who is worthy of consideration when decisions are made. Such a child's self-esteem will be enhanced.

25 ■ When the Schoolhouse Is Open, Be There

When your child's school holds an open house, be there!

You are likely to miss some of your children's Little League games. You may not make it to every school play, concert, or art show. You may not make it to the PTA meeting when the band plays.

But, *be there* when you have an opportunity to talk to your child's teacher or view your child's classroom. That goes for both parents, not just Mom.

Why is this so important?

For one reason, open house happens only once or twice a year. Your child knows that and is not likely to understand your failure to attend when you've had plenty of time to plan for it.

For another reason, open house is the one opportunity your child has to share with you the place where he or she spends most of the waking hours outside your home.

For a third reason, open house is your child's opportunity to show you success in a "world" other than home. It's his or her chance to show off a little, with a teacher for support.

Your child will no doubt show you work on a bulletin board, a project that he or she has helped to build, or a class experiment. That's a way for your child to say, "See, Dad, I'm a part of this group. Is that OK with you? It feels good to me, but is it OK with you? My work is on display as being good. Do you think it's good, too?"

In addition to open house, make your best effort to go to every teacher-parent conference. If your child's teacher or principal asks to see you, make an appointment as quickly as you can.

By visiting with your child's teacher, not only will you learn important facts about your child, and in some cases nip problems in the bud, you will also be sending a message to your child that you care about his or her school life and intellectual growth. You convey as well the message that you are one hundred percent behind the idea of school, the role of teachers and principals, and the business of learning. You are saying to your child, "I value your mind. I want to see you learn everything you can learn. I want you to be as smart as you can be and to accomplish as much as you can."

Whenever you are able, respond to teacher requests for "parent help." That may mean helping to chaperone a field trip, bringing cupcakes to a class party, or setting up decorations for a school dance.

A child whose parents show an interest in school is a child who places higher value on his or her own ability to learn. And in most cases, a child whose parents are pro-school is a child who does better in school.

26 ■ "When You Were Little"

Every child loves to hear stories in which he or she is the hero or heroine. Telling stories to your child validates your child's existence. It conveys, "I remember this about you. You are important enough for me to remember things you said and did, and things you now say and do."

Tell your child about the funny things he or she said or did as a baby or toddler. Give your child an opportunity to laugh at his or her creativity and wit. Make certain, of course, that you never laugh *at* your child, only *with* him or her.

Tell about times when your child did things that were especially endearing—the tender kiss that your child gave to her grandmother when she saw Grandma in a wheelchair for the first time, or the way your child offered a favorite toy to a visiting friend who was sad to see her mother leave. Give children opportunities to see themselves as giving and unselfish.

Tell about times when your child did something that took courage. Tell your child about the brave way he or she walked into the kindergarten classroom the first time. Tell the story of the cat rescued from under the tool shed. Give your son or daughter opportunity to be the hero or heroine.

Stories are an excellent way to praise your child's abilities, even as you tell about your child's accomplishments. "I remember the time when you were only fourteen-months-old and you walked down the front stairs taking one giant step after another. You always were extremely well coordinated. It's no wonder to me now that you excel at sports."

Interweave what you perceive to be the child's outstanding talents and inherent abilities with a story that exemplifies those traits—and watch the glow!

Tell your child stories that show how your child may have inherited the qualities of respected family members. Give your child a positive sense of family heritage. "On the night we brought home your puppy, I found you fast asleep next to your puppy's box; your arm was right next to the puppy inside the box, and the puppy was curled up against your hand. You had heard the puppy crying and had gone to its side to pet it and let it know it wasn't alone. That reminded me of the night you were asleep on your father's chest as he sat sound asleep in the living room rocker. It seems to me you have your father's soft heart for innocent creatures in need of comfort. I hope you never lose that quality."

Positive stories of your child's childhood give your son or daughter a sense of continuity within and linkage to the lives of others he or she considers important. Such tales convey a sense of parental stability, faithfulness, and steadfastness to a child.

27 ■ Let Your Child Be the Teacher

Give your child opportunities to teach you something that he or she knows but that you don't know. Perhaps nothing gives a child a greater "high" than to know something well enough to teach it to someone he or she loves.

How are you at video games? Let your child teach you a trick or two. Have you read the book your child has just finished reading? Let your child tell you the story. Have you figured out how to operate your new VCR? Your child probably knows. Let him or her show you.

Much of the time you are in the teacher's seat, your child at the learning desk. Turn the tables occasionally, and watch your child take a giant step on the path to self-confidence!

Chances are

- he probably knows how to work all of his toys better than you do.
- she's probably up on all the newest fashion fads far more than you are.

- he's probably more keenly aware of the newest television characters and programs than you are.
- she probably knows the latest slang and teen lingo better than you do.
- he probably knows far more about the other kids in the neighborhood than you know.
- she probably knows how to do more with her hair and nails and make-up than you ever dreamed possible!

Ask your child to teach you something you want to know. And then make a sincere effort to learn. You may not want to know the latest slang phrases so you can use them, but you may want to know what they mean so you can understand your teen. You may not want to know how to apply false fingernails in order to wear them yourself; you can still find the process fascinating.

To be a good "student," you need to stay curious about your child's world. Ask about your child's favorite music and musicians. Ask to see and hear the lyrics of favorite songs! (That's sure to be an eye-opening lesson!) You may want to suggest a night in which you share music. You play songs that were "big" when you were your child's age, let him or her play current favorites.

Take time to listen to your child's observations.

One day John's son, Tim, said with excitement, "There goes a '67 Mustang, Dad!" John replied in surprise, "How did you know that's a '67?" Over the course of the next half-hour, John discovered that Tim could identify virtually every car on the road by make, model, and year. Not only that, but Tim knew which cars were rated most reliable by consumer and car magazines. Guess who John consulted the next time he was in the market for a new company car?

Gina had a formal party to attend—a company Christmas party at a major hotel ballroom. Guess who Gina took along to help her shop for a dress? Her thirteen-year-old daughter! Said Gina, "She's the family expert on fashion. She knows exactly what's in and how to wear it, tie it, curl it, or style it."

Giving your child a chance to be the expert says to your child, "I value what you know. I appreciate your sharing it with me." A child who teaches others is not only confident of the information locked away in his or her mind but also carries the self-esteem of one who is looked to and sought out as a valued instructor.

28 ■ Teach Your Child How to Be "Found"

Teach your child what to do when he or she is lost.

Teach your child how to read a map.

Children who have some grasp of how to get from where they are to where they want to be are less timid, more self-reliant, and more confident about surviving in the "real" world.

Nearly every child will experience at least a brief moment of panic as he or she realizes, "I'm alone!" or "I'm lost!" It can happen any time the child gets momentarily separated from the family or group in the jostle and rush of a crowd.

The first response of a child is usually to call for help—even if it's only a silent, inner shout. The second response is usually to cry. You can help your child know what to do as a third response. Teach your child to take the steps that will help him or her find the way back to the group, to safety, or home.

Teach your younger child what to do if he or she feels lost. The number-one principle your child should remember is to stay put. Assure your child that you will probably soon realize he or she is missing. Explain that because you are taller, you'll probably be able to find him or her even before he or she can spot you. However, you won't be able to search as easily if he or she continues to move around!

Teach your child early to speak his or her name clearly, and to give a full name when asked. Children as young as two- or three-years-old can also learn their address and phone number.

Teach your child *your* name, too. Let your child know that you have a name other than "Mommy" or "Daddy" and that you use that name with other adults.

Teach your child to look for an adult with a badge of some kind. A badge, of course, is readily visible on a law enforcement officer or a security officer. A nametag such as the kind belonging to a store clerk or a receptionist might also be considered a badge. Train your child to say, "I'm lost. Can you help me? My name is _____. I was with _____." Assure your child that getting lost doesn't mean he or she is stupid. And be sure to tell your child *never* to leave an area or get into a car with a stranger, even one with a badge.

Being lost can also mean being off-course. That's when map-reading skills become important.

You can make a map of your yard, your block or apartment complex, your neighborhood, or your favorite park. Have the child identify key landmarks. Then use the map to get from a designated point A to point B. The very activity of creating a map helps your child become more observant of his or her surroundings—a key skill to have if he or she becomes lost.

When you take trips or run errands, occasionally

have your child play the role of navigator. Show your child how to read a map of your city and how to translate two-dimensional directions to the three-dimensional world outside the car window.

As you visit local shopping centers, amusement parks, and zoos, look for the maps often located at entrances or near elevators. Show older children how to find the "you are here" spot and then how to locate where it is that you want to go. When you are entering a mall, park, or large building together, it's a good idea to identify a place where you will meet should you become separated. Deciding on a meeting spot and knowing how to read a map to get there can give children a great deal of confidence in a new environment.

Show your child how to make a simple map from verbal instructions. Also, teach your child how to give directions from a map. Ask your child to make a map of your local supermarket and give directions from it.

Be willing to ask directions when you get off-course. Teach your child by example that there's no fault or embarrassment in asking. Most people are eager to help with directions.

Children who know where they are, where they're going, and where they've been are children who have confidence. Teaching your child how to take and give directions and map-reading skills says to your child, "I value you too much to let you feel lost and helpless. I want you to be found. I want to be with you." A child with high self-esteem is a child who feels "found."

29 ■ Give Your Child Rejection- Coping Skills

Every child at some point will face another child, a sibling perhaps, or even an adult, who will say, "Go away. I don't want to play with you. I don't want you around."

Giving your child some skills to use in coping with rejection is a way of saying to your child, "You are a great person, and you have value even in those moments when you feel other people aren't recognizing you for the fine child you are!"

Explain to your child the reasons why others may reject him or her.

A child may be rejected because the other person or group is engaged in an activity or game. The child may actually be interrupting. He or she is not being rejected as a person but is just being asked to wait. Teach your child to recognize feelings of rejection that arise when he or she tries to draw someone's attention away from something already in progress. Teach your child to say, "Sorry. I'll come back later."

A child may be rejected because of his or her own bad behavior. Encourage your child to admit the fact that his or her misbehavior has alienated others. Teach your child to say, "I'm sorry." When an apology is offered, children are usually forgiving, and play frequently resumes after a few moments.

"But, I didn't do anything!" That's a phrase parents hear frequently. "Perhaps you did and you don't know it" is a good reply. Encourage your child to ask playmates: "Did I do something wrong?" Encourage your child to admit wrongdoing when he or she has hurt another child's feelings.

A child may be rejected because of jealousy on the part of the other child or children. Having someone reject you out of jealousy may be hurtful, but such rejection is usually related to an award you've won, praise or an honor you've received, or new possessions. Such rejection is not usually a rejection of who you are. In many cases, rejection that stems from jealousy is based on something your child has done "right," not something he or she has done wrong. Help your child to recognize this fact.

A child may be rejected simply because the other child is in a bad mood. Something may have happened to throw the other child, or children, into a major snit having nothing to do with your child. The rejecting child may just have been punished, heard bad news, or been rejected him or herself. Encourage your child to give the other child some time and space to regain self-control.

A child may be rejected because another child has been taught incorrectly. A playmate's parents may have instilled prejudices or taught false premises or incorrect facts. A child can generally tell if rejection is based on factors such as race, religion, disability, or income level. Explain to your child that some people are ill-informed, and that the best thing your child can do to teach the rejecting person the truth is to continue to do his or her best, stay cheerful, and be kind.

Your goal is to encourage your child not to internalize rejection. Help your child recognize that some rejections are temporary, some are not your child's fault, and some can be resolved with an apology. Separate rejection that is related to something your child *does* from something that your child *is*.

Teach your child that not all people have the same tastes, likes, dislikes, opinions, valuations, or styles. People are different. Some people will click with your child's personality, creations, and likes and dislikes. Others won't.

One way of helping children cope with rejection is to encourage your child to pray for the offending child or group. Prayer is something positive your child can do in a negative situation. Not only does this type of prayer help a child to feel better emotionally, it provides a more positive framework in which your child might approach the other person in the future.

By giving your child a framework for understanding rejection and skills for coping with rejection, you'll be boosting your child's confidence level. You'll also be helping your child to retain his or her self-esteem when it comes under attack.

30 ■ Your Child, the Giver

Give your child the opportunity to give. The child with self-esteem gives voluntarily. Encouraging your child to be generous even when it isn't his or her idea helps build self-esteem.

The gift may be the time it takes to visit a sick grandparent. It may be raking leaves or holding a ribbon while someone else ties a bow. It may be the sharing of cookies, toys, or clothes.

The hallmarks of a gift are these: the person who receives the gift doesn't ask for it, and the gift is given without any expectation of something in return.

In many cases, you are wisest to suggest, not demand, that your child make a gift. A gift given under "command" isn't really a gift; it's a grudging act of obedience.

Don't, however, let your child use giving as a form of manipulation, which happens when a child comes to expect a gift in return.

Encourage your child to give some gifts that are sacrificial, especially as your child moves into teenage years and is able to understand the value of time and things.

Teach your child to give without pity and as an expression of love, concern, and compassion. Don't let your child look down upon the recipient of his or her gift. Many children are encouraged to give their old toys to poor children. Children who only give their old toys come to believe that poor children are only deserving of old, used-up things.

Teach your child that giving can happen year round, and even spontaneously. One doesn't need to have gift wrapping or ribbons for a gift to be a gift. One doesn't need to wait for birthdays or holidays.

Encourage your child to give gifts of service to those in need, such as a free mowing of the elderly neighbor's front yard, an evening of free babysitting to an aunt who never gets an evening off, or five good backrubs for Dad.

Finally, even as you encourage your child to give, insist that your child tell you in advance what he or she is giving and to whom. You don't want your child walking off with your silverware and giving it to the neighbors down the street; neither do you want your child giving away clothing without your knowing it!

The child who becomes a giver is a child who comes to know, "I can spare some of what I have because I know it won't detract or subtract from who I am. I have value unconnected to things."

No matter the shelflife or the value of the gift, the value of gift-giving is lasting and great!

31 ■ Make Sure Your Child Has Money for Two Phone Calls

One simple and effective way to build confidence in your child is to make certain that he or she always has enough money for at least two phone calls.

You may want to hand-stitch a small Velcro-fastened coin person into your child's coat pocket, add a couple of quarters to the key holder tied to your child's shoes, or hide phone money on your child's bicycle.

Having money for two phone calls assures your child that he or she can reach you, or someone else you designated, in an emergency. (If you have an answering machine, make sure your child knows to wait and to leave a message that tells you where he or she is, what the problem is, what you are to do, and where he or she is going after hanging up the phone.)

Teach your child that if one coin is lost, the second coin should be used to phone an operator by dialing "0." Train your child to say to the operator, "Hello. I'm having trouble. I'm only _____ years old and I need your help. I have only one quarter, and I need to talk to

_____. This is the number I have. But, if they aren't there, I need to be able to call someone else. Will you help me?" A phone operator will be delighted to help a child who is that polite and that organized!

Make sure your child has your home phone number memorized, as well as at least one other number where help is likely to be found. The second number may be the phone number of your employer, a grandmother, your spouse's business, a friend, or someone else available for emergency help. Make certain, also, that your child knows the name of your and your spouse's employer or company.

Stress upon your child the importance of not spending this money. Make sure he or she understands that it's for an emergency and that the money is best "forgotten" unless an emergency arises. Check periodically to make certain that the coins are where they should be!

Teach your child that he or she can always call 911 (if that number is available in your city or area) or an operator to summon help. Make certain your child knows that the 911 number summons a policeman, fireman, or an ambulance driver and that it should be used *only* when such people are needed.

A child armed with the potential for two phone calls is a child who can generally turn a bad situation into a good one. A child who knows when and whom to call for help is a child who feels less alone and less fearful.

32 ■ Encourage Your Child to Memorize

In the course of attending school, most children will learn the Pledge of Allegiance. Very few schools, however, will teach your child to memorize anything in its entirety beyond that—a skill and practice that seems to have gone by the wayside in this century.

The memorization of a poem, quotation, or phrase helps your child focus on words and the ways in which language is structured and used. The child who hears language—through such activities as being read to by loving adults—is a child who will grow up with a greater love for and facility with language. The same holds true for a child who speaks words in an order that he or she might not otherwise put them. The child's awareness of how words might be used is enhanced. He or she learns new words and has a greater awareness of how words can be put together into phrases. And often, the child comes to the conclusion that using language can be fun.

The material memorized can often be recalled almost by "instinct" during times when it is needed or seems appropriate. Even if your child doesn't utter the phrases, the memorized words will often float through his or her mind, reinforcing the concepts conveyed by the words. This is especially true for proverbs and songs that have been taught as capsules of important truths.

The recitation of a memorized piece is an "accomplishment" for a child. Recitation is an example of a child's ability to learn; it says to others, "I memorized this. I know it. Nobody can rob me of it."

What should you have your child memorize?

Have your child memorize things that are important or meaningful to you. What your child memorizes then become a bond of shared information between the two of you. The content of that bond may be Scriptures, proverbs, your favorite poems, or rhymes you learned as a child. You may select something simply for the beauty of the words or because of the impact the words had when you first understood their message. When appropriate, tell your child why the piece or song is meaningful to you.

Have your child memorize prose, poems, or songs that convey a message that you want your child to incorporate into the fabric of his or her character. The piece memorized may be part of a patriotic speech, a passage from a famous sermon, a chapter from one of the Gospels, a poem about right and wrong.

Have your child memorize some things that are simply fun to say or sing. Share with your child the fact that words can be fun; songs can be silly. Some words are simply meant to help us feel good and to bring a smile to our faces. Give your child something "happy" to remember when feeling sad.

Make certain that your children have certain facts memorized at an early age. Make sure your child knows his or her full name, street address and city, phone number, parent's names, parents' employers, the name of his or her school and teachers. You might want to quiz your child on a fairly regular basis until you are certain that your child can respond quickly and automatically with key information.

Use repetition to teach your child to memorize. Break down long pieces into smaller units that can be memorized and then strung together.

Once a child has successfully memorized a piece, help the child keep that piece memorized and in the "active file" through repetition every few weeks or months.

Give your child a verbal heritage, a language inheritance, and the confidence that comes from "saying a piece." Give your child the self-esteem boost that comes from realizing that he or she is being trusted with an important family or cultural tradition!

33 ■ Give Your Child Freedom to Explore

Give your child the freedom to explore the world, within the bounds of health and safety. In so doing, you'll be giving your child the confidence that comes from knowing, "I don't need to be afraid of a new experience."

Many parents hold on too tightly. Others don't care enough. Where is the fine line of a balanced approach? In a broad sense, that line can be summed up in one phrase: Keep small children within eyesight or earshot (whenever you are outside your home).

Keep your children within eyesight or earshot until you are certain they are near another adult that cares about them and will assume responsibility for them.

Watch your child walk to the school bus until he or she gets on it. Watch your child enter the door of the Sunday school classroom. Check on your child every few minutes as he or she plays outside in the yard— even if it's just a glance through a window or a pause to listen for the sound of his or her voice. Watch your child in the park, even if you are seated several yards away on a bench. Make certain that a playmate's parent is home and that the parent knows your child is coming to visit *before* you drive away.

Does this take effort? Yes. Responsible parenting always takes effort.

One of the milestones of my childhood came the day that our family went to Disneyland and my parents said, "You and your brother can do whatever you want for the next hour. You both have wristwatches. Here are your ticket books. Meet us right here in an hour. If you do that, we'll know we can trust you to be on your own for another hour or so."

Unknown to us, Mom and Dad followed us from a distance for the next hour, to make certain we didn't stray from our instructions or fail to wait patiently in lines. My brother and I felt great freedom and a great deal of responsibility for being "on our own" for a while. We probably took greater care of each other and showed more constraint than we would have had our parents been right at our sides! We were careful to return on time. And, we were both proud that we had done something without adult supervision. It was only years later that we learned that Mom and Dad had been a hundred feet away at all times. We were within their eyesight, even if they weren't within ours.

Is your child wanting to be alone with friends at the fair? Watch from afar. Does your fourth-grade son want to walk to school with his friends? Watch from afar at least until his feet hit school property. Does your ten-year-old daughter want to shop with her friends at the mall? Shop, too, and keep track of her from afar.

When do you stop watching? As your child enters teen years and proves himself or herself to be trustworthy, you can decrease the vigilance. It is still your responsibility, however, to know where your teen is and where he or she can be reached by phone.

Even as you are watching, encourage your child to explore his or her world. Suggest that he or she climb that tree, try the slide, walk out to the end of the dock and look for fish, and run ahead of you on the beach to explore the tidal pools. Let your child try the scales for a penny and take a blood pressure reading for a quarter.

Let your child find things for you and do things that carry responsibility. "Jimmy, will you please run and get a quart of milk while I wait in the check-out line with the cart." Or, "Caitlyn, will you please run out and put this coin in the parking meter for me."

By encouraging the independent discovery of new things, you're giving your child the confidence that, indeed, he or she is able to learn and cope with new experiences and information.

The child who is given the freedom to roam, to get dirty, to pick up frogs, and to jump from swings is the child who is going to get a bruise now and then. But this is also a child whose spirit and imagination will be allowed to soar.

A child with high self-esteem is a child who believes he or she can conquer something new even before the attempt—and even if he or she fails at it initially!

34 ■ Teach Your Child Basic Self-Defense Skills

Provide your child with basic self-defense skills. This is important not only for maintaining your child's self-confidence and self-esteem, but for insuring your child's life.

In our society today, children need to have a defensive strategy for resisting drug dealers, abusers, cultists, and kidnappers.

Drug dealers, or any persons who attempt to seduce your child into trying alcohol, cigarettes, pills, or other chemicals, must be shunned.

Abusers inflict sexual, physical, or emotional injury. If a person is consistently attempting to exert power over your child (the person's behavior may be causing a change in your child's personality), your child is experiencing a serious form of abuse.

This is not to say that parents who punish their children for misbehavior are abusers. A spanking may "hurt" a child, but that is a physical hurt that goes away quickly and can and should be compensated with an equal dose of love and tenderness. Abuse never has a good excuse and never a legitimate cause.

Cultists may attempt to woo your child into a secret

or exclusive group, from which you, the parent, are barred. Most cults offer young people acceptance into a group that asks the son or daughter to reject parents, lie to them, or overtly rebel against them.

Kidnappers attempt to abduct your child or keep your child from getting home to you. It's no longer enough to teach your child never to talk to strangers. Statistics show that the person most likely to do physical or emotional harm to children is an adult that the children know, even love.

Talk to your children about the tactics that a potential kidnapper or abuser may use. In most cases, the initial approach will be a friendly one. Often, your child will be offered something fun, exciting, or appealing.

Teach your child specific times to say no.

- if someone your child doesn't know offers him or her anything to eat or smoke.
- if someone offers your child any type of pill.
- if someone your child doesn't know well offers a ride home.
- if someone touches your child on any part of the body that is considered "private."
- if someone tells your child not to show or tell you something, no matter what the reason or the secret.

Beyond "just say no" your child needs to be taught to take two additional steps:

One. "Run away as fast as you can." Teach your child

not to negotiate, discuss, or argue with a person who offers gifts or makes advances!

Two. "Come tell me what has happened and tell me *immediately*—no matter what the other person says or threatens." Assure your child that a threat the other person may have made is not a good enough excuse to keep from telling you what has happened.

Above all, establish a relationship with your child in which he or she can always come to you with a question, a hurt, or a concern. When your child does come, always assume that what you hear is the truth.

Don't dismiss your child's hurts, concerns, or questions. Say to your child, "What that person said or did is *not* acceptable. I'm angry that this has happened to you. I'm glad you told me about it." Say it with a hug.

If a child tells you that he or she has been abused by a person, by all means don't allow that child to be with that person until you've sorted out the full extent of the abuse and the abuser has been confronted. (In many cases, you'll want to call authorities to do the confronting!)

Talk to your child about drugs, explaining the difference between the terms *drugs* and *medicines.*

Talk to your child about the dangers of child abuse and of your child's right to be treated with respect by adults.

Your child should be able to cope with these topics if you couch your discussion in terms of your love and desire to see him or her protected and safe.

35 ■ Allow Your Child to Have Significant Others

Encourage your child to have relationships with other trusted adults from whom you believe your child can gain information, receive love, and regard as a role model for positive behaviors. Such a "significant other" will help you build your child's self-esteem. Such a person will give your child confidence that he or she won't be alone in the world should something happen to you.

Children need to have assurance that they will be cared for should their parents die. Children may be exposed at an early age to death and to separation from parents. They wonder, and often wonder aloud, "What will happen to me if you aren't here?" Be sure you can give your child a concrete answer. Part of your responsibility as a loving parent is to make sure your child does have a place to go and someone who will care for him or her in the event that you become incapacitated or die.

On an everyday level, encourage your child to have a good relationship with grandparents, aunts, and uncles. This is a real challenge in homes broken apart by divorce; recognize that no matter how much pain you have felt, your child still needs to have a relationship with your spouse and his or her family members. To rob your child of half of his or her extended family is to rob your child of many invaluable memories and experiences. Children won't understand why they have been cut off from a loving grandfather or grandmother just because daddy or mommy went away. You will only be deepening a child's sense of loss by forcing a separation from your former spouse's relatives.

One of the hallmarks of a significant other for your child will be the fact that this person *wants* to spend time with your child and wants to be a part of his or her life. Look for those adults who truly enjoy being with your child, and with whom your child enjoys spending time. Foster those relationships by

- allowing your child to spend time with this person.
- encouraging your child to talk over problems with this person.
- helping your child to choose gifts for this person, and to show gratitude for gifts received from him or her.
- regarding this person as an extended part of your family in your conversations and activities.

Encourage your child to invite his or her significant others to school plays, soccer games, youth choir concerts, and other events. Invite the person to participate in family outings.

Don't be hurt, and don't let your child's feelings be hurt, if your child's "older friend" can't accept all such invitations. "Maybe next time" is a good response to teach children in such situations.

Let your child know the limitations of authority and responsibility that a significant other has over him. (Talk that over with the significant other, too!)

Do have periodic conversations with your child's godparents, aunts and uncles, or grandparents about your child. Let them know a little of what your child is experiencing and with what he or she is struggling. Let them know your child's accomplishments and disappointments. Let them know about his or her activities and interests. This will give these significant others clues as to how to talk to your child, what to listen for, and what to buy for Christmas presents!

Children who have at least one or two other adults to whom they can turn for advice, friendship, understanding, and hugs have confidence that they are valued beyond the immediate family. They know they are not alone, even when parents are unavailable. Give your child that kind of boost to his or her esteem and confidence level!

36 ■ Zip the Critical Comments

When your child hears you criticize people that he or she loves, resentment about your comments may result. When a child hears you criticize people that *you* supposedly love, he or she begins to question your claims about love. Your child is apt to think, "If Mom says that about Grandma, and at the same time says she loves Grandma, then what does 'love' really mean. What does she mean when she says she loves and values me?"

Your child may also wonder, "What does Dad say about me behind my back? Does he tell me he loves me and values me to my face, and then tell others he hates me and that I'm not worth anything? Can I trust what my Dad says to me as being what he really believes?"

Don't criticize your child's friends in his or her presence.

Don't criticize an absent parent in your child's presence (whether he or she is away at work or out of the home owing to divorce or separation).

Don't criticize your own friends or relatives in your child's presence.

Does this mean you should only say good things about people to the exclusion of telling the truth?

No. For example, if your child's other parent is in prison, your child needs to know that fact. Don't lie to your child by saying that he or she is away on business. Someone else will tell your child the truth—count on it. Then you'll be faced not only with the truth of your spouse's condition, but also with the fact of your own lie! You can tell your child that Mom or Dad has been put in prison for a very serious mistake. You don't need to tell all the details, but don't tell your child that your spouse is a dirty, rotten, no-good scoundrel beyond redemption.

You can tell your child that you really don't like the way a playmate dresses. Couch your comments in terms of "that's not my taste" or "I don't think that's the best style for her." But don't say, your friend is "bad" or "slovenly" or that "she dresses like a slut." And don't say, "I think Rod's parents are crazy for letting him wear his hair that way."

In sum, you may point out to your child certain *behaviors* of which you don't approve, but don't downgrade the character, reputation, or personality of the friend! Separate deeds from personhood.

Criticism of others can do serious damage to your child's own confidence and esteem. Be aware that such criticism can confuse your child. Work to avoid criticizing others in the presence of your child.

37 ■ Don't Make Idle Threats

Harassing your child with idle threats is an extremely effective way of tearing down confidence and destroying self-esteem. Idle threats instill fear in a child, and fear eats away at confidence. Idle threats also cause your child to feel alienation. "If Mom is threatening me, she must not really value my safety or wellbeing."

Not only do idle threats cause fear and disciplinary inconsistency, they destroy your reputation as a truth-speaker.

An idle threat is not a fact. That's critically important to recognize. It is *not* an idle threat to say to your child, "If you do that one more time, I'm going to take you out of this room, and we will discuss your punishment." It is *not* an idle threat to say to your child, "That is the third time you have willfully disobeyed me today. I am going to spank you when we get home." Those are not idle threats if you follow through and do what you have just said you were going to do! Those are statements of what will happen. They are declarations of consequence.

It is an idle threat, however, for you to say, *"Daddy's going to spank you for that, if you do it"* and then to have no spanking from Daddy after the bad deed is done. Not following through leads your child to think, *I don't know when I can trust Daddy to tell the truth. Maybe he doesn't tell me the truth about who I am or how much he cares about me. Maybe his promises aren't true either.*

If an idle threat is not a fact—because the threat never becomes a reality—then the idle threat is not true. If not true, it is a lie.

Some parents threaten their children with monsters that will rise up from under the bed to "get them" if they get out of bed without asking permission.

Some threaten their children with bogeymen who live just beyond the boundaries you've established for your child and who will "get them," if they stray from the backyard or climb out of the window at night.

Some threaten their children with abandonment. "I'm going to leave you here if you don't come right away."

Tell the *truth* to your child. Follow through on what you say you are going to do. Give what you promise. Punish according to the rules you've established. Let your yes be yes and your no mean no.

The child who is told the truth knows what to believe about him or her self. That's a critical factor in the formation of your child's self-esteem.

38 ■ Give Your Child Advance Warning

Whenever possible, prepare your child for new situations and new experiences. Boost your child's confidence level by providing "advance warning."

Prepare your child for a new house. Talk about the move, and if possible, drive through the new neighborhood and tour the new house. If you are house hunting and are closing in on a decision, take your child along. Let him or her feel a part of the decision.

Help orient your child to a new school. Go to the school in advance of your child's first day and walk around the buildings and the playground. Talk about the fun times that your child will have at the new school. If possible, meet your child's teacher and go to his or her classroom.

Explain to your child how the new school operates—about bells, recess, lunchbreaks, and the different subjects that will be studied. Talk over any differences between the new school and the old one. Discuss the fact that the class schedules and the expectations of teachers may be different, too.

Prepare your child for the first trip to camp. I can remember my parents taking me into the mountains one Saturday afternoon in the spring to show me the campgrounds where I'd be spending a week that coming summer. We drove around the cabins and walked around the pond and even peered into the windows of the dining hall.

During the next several weeks, I found it easy to imagine "going to camp" and when the time actually came, I boarded the bus without fear and with a great deal of confidence.

Help your child prepare for his or her first stage performance. If at all possible, before that first Christmas program, school play, or recital, walk through the event with your child. Give your child an opportunity to be on the real stage and to look out at the audience area. Give your child an opportunity to rehearse in front of a group, even if it's just the family in the living room with your child standing on a chair or footstool!

Prepare your child for any first-time experience. Whenever possible, anticipate your child's questions as he or she faces a new experience. It may be an overnight visit to a friend's house, a slumber party, a dance, first communion service or the first time your child is in a wedding.

Confidence. Self-esteem. The child who is given advance warning is a child who feels ready for a challenge and who knows "I'm valued enough to be told what's going on. I don't need to be scared of new things. Mom and Dad think I can handle this situation, and therefore, I probably can!"

39 ■ Help Your Child Develop Failure-Coping Skills

No matter how much you prepare a child for an experience, and no matter how many times your child may have done something correctly in the past, your child is going to have times when he or she fails.

- He's going to miss the basket at the buzzer, and his team will lose by a point.
- She's *not* going to be among those named as a top-ten finalist.
- He's going to score fewer points than anticipated on the exam.
- She's going to trip on stage.

Failures are a part of life. Teaching your child how to handle failure is one of the best lessons you can give. To do this effectively you must separate your child's failed performance from your child's success at being your son or daughter.

Children fail at things they try to do. Don't just say to

your child, "Better luck next time." Instead, say, "I'm proud of you for what you did. You had the courage to get up in front of a group of people. You had the desire to do that project and do your best. I'm proud of that."

What about those instances when your child tries and fails at something because he or she hadn't practiced and wasn't prepared as well as he or she could have been?

You can use the incident to talk about what can be done in the future to avoid such a disappointment. Talk to your child as if you are in a debriefing session.

Above all, separate the idea that your child "failed" from any notion that your child is a "failure."

Be especially alert for those moments when your child says, "I just don't understand this subject" or "I just can't seem to get the right answers to these problems." Your child may need some special tutoring or additional help. In some cases, your child may have a learning disability that has gone undetected.

Often when a child says, "I just can't do it" it means, "I can't do it as well as the next guy." If this is the case, talk to your child about ways to improve past performance, talk in terms of your own child's willingness to try, desire to succeed, and the effort he or she is willing to put into the activity.

A child who learns to view failure as a passing, temporary glitch in the "system," and who believes that failures can be overcome, is a child who knows he or she is a "success just waiting to happen."

40 ■ Make Sure Your Child Has a Savings Account

Help your child at an early age to start and build a savings account. Give your child an opportunity to earn money and add to the account on a regular basis.

At some point in elementary school, nearly all children learn to define their own socioeconomic status. They know they are richer than some people and poorer than others. A savings account can give your child the feeling, "I'm not as bad off as people may think. I've got some wealth they don't know about!"

A regular pattern of saving teaches your child delayed gratification. Children are often willing to forego fads, if they are saving for something specific and know that they have money accumulating toward that goal. A child who wants a car someday, and who knows that he can buy one if he saves just one dollar a week in an interest-bearing account, is a child less likely to waste money on alcohol, junk food, or video games.

Give your child purchasing goals to shoot for, something to save for. Don't buy everything for your child. A child has the right to expect you to provide for basic needs but should not expect you to provide all of his whims and wishes. Some items do make wonderful surprise gifts (for example, a stereo or telephone), but luxury items often have greater value to your child if you let him or her earn them, plan for them, and anticipate them.

Earning and saving money is a process that builds in your child an understanding that work and effort have value that can be measured. Give your child opportunities to earn money. Always include a savings requirement. Even within a savings account, you may want to differentiate between savings that can be tapped for luxury purchases and savings that are longterm (for college or for a "home of your own" someday).

From time to time, discuss your child's finances. Talk about the wisdom of purchasing a savings bond, for example. Reflect on how many hours it takes to earn certain things. Many children grow up thinking that money is somehow magically available to their parents; they have little concept that Dad and Mom earn their money and that a good wage is not easy to come by.

Going to the bank, dealing with bank books, and balancing accounts gives your child the confidence that comes from managing money and dealing with an important institution.

I am frequently amazed at the number of adults who don't know how to make a budget and don't know how to balance a checkbook. Teach your child those skills. Decide together how he or she is going to budget an allowance or earnings, and what percentage is to be saved. Take your child to the bank. Let your child listen in on your basic transactions and become familiar with financial terms.

Finally, consider these do's and don'ts about your child's money.

- Never encourage your child to put money into something risky. A child can become very discouraged if he or she loses money in the stock market; (so can adults, for that matter!)
- Never borrow money from your children. They won't understand and may not readily forgive your inability to pay or your forgetfulness in repaying the loan.
- Do encourage your teenage child to have a checking account. Teach your teen how to write a check and how to keep track of deposits.

Give your child the confidence that comes from earning, saving, and managing money. Give your child the opportunity to make financial decisions and to learn financial procedures. He or she will grow into an adult that knows, "Mom and Dad thought enough of me to prepare me for the day when I'd be self-supporting and on my own."

41 ■ Try Something New for Both of You

Be adventuresome with your child. Try out activities that are new to both of you.

Trying something new gives your child the opportunity to see you as a fellow explorer in life. Your child can learn important lessons by watching how *you* handle new situations.

The new experience may be a new restaurant or cuisine. Hattie and Will, two young friends of mine, recently went with me to a Lebanese restaurant. They nixed the humus tahini, but raved about the tabouli and cabbage rolls. Now they know about Lebanese food and will order from a strange-sounding menu.

Encourage your children to try new foods. You never know what may take them someday to China or Africa, where they'll need to be willing to try foods they've never seen or heard about!

The new experience may be a concert or theatrical performance. Youngsters Allen and Jon weren't at all sure what to expect from an afternoon at a performance they couldn't even pronounce. They came away in awe at the staging and music of *Les Misérables.* They are now avid theater-goers and have found a new interest beyond movies and rock concerts.

Just a few years ago, my father and I went to our first rodeo. It was fun to make a new memory together. One never gets too old for new adventures.

The new experience may be a trip to another city, state, or country. Build confidence in your child by traveling with him or her and showing him or her new areas of our nation or world. Not only will your child have the benefit of seeing new things and experiencing new customs and languages, but he or she will learn how to pack a suitcase, how to handle emergencies far from home, how to deal with motion sickness or jetlag, how to communicate with new people, how to order from menus, how to adjust to new beds, and how to get on and off a plane, train, boat, or bus. Those may not seem like necessary skills but the broader capacity of flexibility and adaptability is a vital one.

The new experience may be attending a church of a different denomination. When I was eight, our Camp Fire Girl chapter went on a field trip to one of the California missions. Of the dozen girls in the group, only one was Catholic. We were grateful that she knew what to do when we found ourselves in the middle of a morning prayer service. Never before had this group of little Protestant girls found themselves in a church where kneeling rails, genuflection, and missals were part of the service. We were suddenly in the midst of an adventure together that was just as exciting as any overnight campout. (We also learned that day that Catholics and Protestants may differ in style, but that otherwise, they really aren't all that far apart in most of their basic beliefs. That was a major revelation to us all!)

Sharing new experiences with your child lets your child know that the adventure into the unknown can be exciting. The trick is to explore safely, cautiously, and to choose your unknowns wisely!

The new experiences you share with your child will form a bond between the two of you. They will become a treasure of memories and a rich source of conversation all your life. You will be saying to your child, "I enjoy being with you. I value you as a fellow explorer in life. I want you to be able to see this world as a challenge that can be confronted and enjoyed, and I want to help you learn how to get the most out of life." A child who learns that lesson is a child who has acquired self-esteem.

42 ■ Teach Your Child to Fix Breaks and Rips

Things break. The first tendency of a parent is to fix the break, mend the torn garment, put the arm of the doll back on, sew on the button, or clean up the mess on the floor.

Some parents become angry at the child for carelessness. While that may be warranted on occasion, a parent also needs to be aware that some mishaps in life truly are accidents.

Rather than be angry or resort to remedying the situation yourself, try a third option. Let your child repair the damage or clean up the results as best he or she can.

Small children can learn to use a sponge to clean up spilled milk. They may not get it all, but let them make a genuine effort. Older children can learn how to sweep up broken glass.

Through the years, make it a point to teach your child certain fix-it skills. Teach your child how to sew on a button and how to put in a hem. Teach your child how to use a hammer and how to glue things together. Teach your older child how to replace light bulbs and fuses.

Again, not all skills are appropriate for young children. Teach your child skills as they become appropriate to his or her level of manual dexterity, muscle coordination, and sense of judgment.

When mechanical items break, encourage your child to explore with you the potential for repairing them. Don't just discard it with the assumption that it can't be fixed or that you can't fix it! Have a home-repairs book on your bookshelf and consult it. Let your child take on the challenge of replacing a transistor or screwing together pieces that may have come apart.

Teach your child the difference between items that are worn, and items that are worn-out. Some of the most valuable antiques on the market today are items that are well-worn, but which still have value.

Teach your child the difference between items that are worth fixing and items that should be replaced. Count the cost over the long run. It may be cheaper to buy a new vacuum cleaner, for example, than to continually repair an old one. Explain your reasoning to your child for fixing or replacing an item.

The child who learns to fix things learns that when things break they often can be fixed. This is a lesson that translates to relationships fairly easily as a child matures.

Give your child the opportunity to fix things and to use things that have been repaired. He'll have a greater appreciation for the way things are made and the way they work.

43 ■ Share Your Hopes

Tell your child what you hope for in his or her life. Share with your child what you hope for your child for all eternity.

Nearly all parents hope their children will have

- long life and health.
- their material needs met.
- friends and loving relationships.
- work that is fulfilling.
- noble character traits.

Parents the world over hope that their children will always have enough good food to eat and clean water to drink, a safe place to sleep, warmth in the cold, relief in the heat, and comfortable shelter.

Tell your children you hope they will have good friends, with whom they can talk, pray and share experiences; coworkers, with whom they can accomplish goals; and mentors, from whom they may learn.

Whether framed in terms of a career or an avocation, most parents hope for their children the fulfillment found in the completion of worthy tasks or goals.

Every parent will no doubt help define the values his or her child will carry into the world and apply to life. Honesty, fidelity, kindness, patience, peace, joy, love, humility, confidence and self-esteem are among the traits nearly every parent hopes for his or her child. Compliance with the laws of the land, patriotism, voluntary service—these, too, are valueable traits. Share with your child the type of person you hope he or she will be: cool-headed in emergencies, compassionate in tragedies, angry at injustice, bold to speak for the weak, eager to help in times of need, and quick to respond to the hurts of others.

Share, too, your deepest desires for your child's spiritual growth. Lou and Mindy travel a great deal with their children. On long car trips they sometimes ask their children, "What do you suppose our lives will be like five hundred years from now?" They imagine heaven and the things they will each be doing and saying. They discuss the relationship between what they do now and the life they anticipate enjoying later. They also talk seriously about the importance of doing certain things and taking certain stands now for the sake of life on earth. They have helped their children, over those miles, to become adept at voicing a theology, framing a worldview, and forging a personal philosophy for living.

Many of your hopes and aspirations can be shared by wrapping your ideas around simple everyday activities. "I'm so glad you were honest in telling me the truth. Lying has terrible consequences—people go to prison for lying, some people destroy their families and their marriages because they lie, some people end up in mental institutions because they make lying a pattern in their lives. I don't want any of those things to happen to you."

Don't pontificate. Don't preach. Don't harp. Don't nag. A paragraph of mom-philosophy, a sentence or two of dad-theology can go along way if spoken sincerely, at a time when you and your child are alone and you both are focused on communicating with each other. Nearly everything you say can be understood by your child, even a rebellious, angry teenager, if you don't *demand* that your child follow your lead or agree with you without question. Confront him or her with issues and options that you hope he or she will ponder or an idea or opinion that you hope he or she will weigh carefully.

A child whose parents share their deepest goals and hopes for his or her life is a child who says, "Mom thinks I can experience this. Dad thinks I can be a person who bears these qualities. They have hope for my future; they believe I will become a solid citizen and a loving and generous adult." When *you* value a child's future, the child will value his or her own future too.

44 ■ Tell Your Child about Sex

The child who is told the "facts of life" within the context of a value system is a child who knows, "Mom and Dad trust me with this information; they value me as a person, and they can tell I'm growing up."

When should you tell your child about sex?

Before someone else does. If you don't talk to your child about sex, be assured that someone else will, and chances are, that someone else will be a peer or an older child who doesn't have all the facts. You'll then have to sort out and undo myths even before you can share facts.

Don't wait for your child to have the classes on "sex education" offered at school. Sex education does not, and cannot address, the "rights and wrongs" associated with sexual behavior; neither will a sex education teacher tell your child when and what kinds of sexual behavior are appropriate.

It's important that you, as a parent, address the physiological changes that boys and girls experience during puberty. It's important that you be the one to explain the differences in anatomy between men and women and that you be the one who tells your child about sexual intercourse.

Bear in mind that a discussion about sexual activity and sexual desires should not be a one-time discussion. It should be an ongoing dialogue you have with your child from the time he or she is about three years old— that is, when your child becomes aware that boys and girls have different body parts—until your son or daughter is an adult. Make certain you refer to various body parts by name. Avoid slang or vulgar expressions.

Make certain you share early with your child those parts of the body that should be considered "private" and which should be protected from intrusion or abuse.

When you discuss sexual functions and sexual behavior, include a discussion about birth control and safe sex. Be sure you also know the facts about AIDS and other sexually transmitted diseases. You need to share this information with your child prior to adolescence.

Many parents find visual aids a help, such as charts, a three-dimensional model (such as the "Invisible Man" and "Invisible Woman" models that show anatomical organs), or dolls. You should be the first person to show your child a condom. When talking about sex, speak objectively.

Answer your child's questions as best you can, and if you are unsatisfied with your answer or your ability to come up with an answer, admit to your child, "I need some time to think about how best to explain that to you." Give yourself a day or two to think it through and then, at an appropriate moment, come back to your child with the answer.

You may not ever be comfortable talking about sex with your child. Take it upon yourself, then, to get information and to make sure your child reads it. Many parents find it easier to talk about sex with their child if the child already has accurate information.

One couple I know had a jar set up in the corner of their kitchen. They invited their children to put into it their toughest questions. They labeled the jar "Dad Stumpers and Mom Puzzlers." The parents assured their children that no questions would be discarded or dismissed as unimportant and that all questions would be answered to the best of their ability. Sometimes the parents went to the library to find a book that would give their children the answers. One night a month the family discussed problems, made up a master calendar of events, reached decisions, and handled the questions from the jar. In the context of a matter-of-fact, agenda-based meeting, these parents found that even difficult or otherwise embarrassing questions could be discussed without giggles, blushing, or cute remarks. In fact, the parents themselves sometimes "planted" questions into the jar in order to make certain that some topics were covered!

Share with your child what sexual behaviors are appropriate, under what conditions and with whom, and give reasons why. Let your child know what you think about holding hands, kissing, nudity, fondling, and intercourse. Talk to your child about the difference between love and sexual acts.

One father told me he considered it his obligation to "line proof" his daughter. "We've made it something of a game we call 'The Lines Guys Use.' She's not going to be an easy mark, believe me!" As part of their discussions down through the years, this father discovered that he and his daughter were exploring a number of differences in the ways men and women communicate. He recently told me, "We've got a new game going. It's called 'What He Means, What She Means.' I think I'm learning as much as she is! Men and women really do communicate in different ways!"

Your child is going to face a great deal of pressure to engage in sexual activity. Recognize that fact early. Regard your child's sex education just as you would your child's education in any other area: deal with questions in a straight-forward, unemotional way.

Children who can talk openly with their parents about sexual behavior feel that they have been let in on one of the main secrets of life. Children who know early on how they are created feel a certain degree of continuity between ancestors and future heirs. Such children feel they have a "place" in the culture and a role in the scheme of a family's history.

45 ■ Give Your Child an Inheritance

Leave something to your child. A child who receives an inheritance is a child who knows that his or her parents were thinking of the future, were considering his or her feelings, and expressing their love even after death.

The child who is excluded from a family inheritance is a child who feels an ache that can never truly be comforted, and experiences a wound that can never truly be healed.

Leaving an inheritance takes advance planning. So, plan! Decide what it is that you hope to leave your child.

An inheritance need not be money alone, although money is not to be discounted.

One couple I know has set the goal of providing as an inheritance for their three children: a college education, an automobile by the time the child is eighteen years old, and the downpayment for a home. They consider this a "living inheritance"—something they will "leave" their children while they themselves are still alive. Now, they aren't committed, necessarily, to new cars, private schools, or mansions. They are committed to expressing to their children that, as parents, they not only desire to help their children grow to adulthood, but that they want to help launch their children into adulthood by providing assistance they believe to be important for a young adult's success. Furthermore, they have told their children nothing of their plans. Working toward these goals is something of a secret mission they share.

Parents may even want to give a portion or the bulk of the inheritance while they are still alive. That gives them an opportunity to watch their children enjoy the inheritance and to be available for answers about the origin of some items, the ways in which some stock portfolios might best be managed, or the meaning behind gifts of a more personal or sentimental nature.

Heirloom-quality and hand-crafted gifts are one way of giving your child a portion of his or her inheritance from an early age. Needlepoint and embroidered gifts may rest on bookshelves, antique dolls may be displayed in a glass cabinet, a passed-down-through-the-family cradle may hold teddy bears in the corner of a child's room. A close friend was given her grandmother's doilies, which she backed with squares of bright jewel-toned silk and converted into pillows. Heirloom and handmade items are gifts of time, love, and family that give a child a sense that he or she is being "gifted" with heritage; later, the child will value the gifts even more as examples of Mom or Dad's trust.

An inheritance displays a great vote of parental confidence to a child—it is an irreplaceable, unduplicatable gift!

46 ■ Teach Children to Take Responsibility for Their Actions

Children who are forced to take responsibility for their own actions know, "Mom and Dad consider me capable of acting on my own, and they count me as a valuable individual who has the ability to stand on my own two feet and face the consequences—good and bad."

When your child breaks the neighbor's window with a baseball, insist that your child render an apology and help pay for the replacement of the window. Now, you may certainly go with your young child to the neighbor's front door, and you may require that your child only come up with a part of the payment. But, at whatever age the accident occurs, don't "cover" for your child.

When your teenager has a fender-bender, insist that he or she help pay for the damages and help out with any increase in your automobile insurance that may result.

When your child rips a neighbor child's shirt in the course of playing tag, go with your child to the neighbor and discuss amends.

Saying "I'm sorry" may be retribution enough. At other times, your child may need to restore or replace the damaged item.

When you dismiss a child's mistakes or bad behavior in the presence of a third person, you are sending the signal to your child, "I don't think that was important." When you cover for your child with a third party—or take the blame on yourself—you are saying, "I'll always be there to bail you out." Neither approach helps your child develop a sense of responsibility, and both lead to self-justifying behavior.

Punishing your child for something done against another person is not a sufficient response in teaching your child responsibility. A spanking may help teach your child not to play baseball in the front yard. It may help the child learn how to avoid breaking a window in the future, and thus, avoid another spanking. But, it will not mend the breech with your neighbor that your child will feel intuitively.

I recently spoke with a woman who said, "I stole a candy bar from Mr. Crabb's store when I was nine years old. My mother found out and spanked me hard. Believe me, I never stole anything again. But, for the next twenty years I couldn't look Mr. Crabb in the eye when I went into his store. Looking back, I wish my mother had required me to go back and apologize to Mr. Crabb and pay for the candy bar. I think I would have felt that the slate of my crime had been truly wiped clean. By his not knowing, I was never able to receive his forgiveness."

When children takes responsibility and makes restitution they come out stronger by facing errors and working through them.

When children face up to the damage or problems they have created, they have the opportunity to ask and receive forgiveness from others. They may then experience the emotionally healing balm of forgiveness granted.

Children who are required to own up to their mistakes do not have to live with the guilt born of secret misdeeds.

Children with confidence can face up to sins, repent of them, and seek forgiveness. Children with high self-esteem know they have been forgiven.

47 ■ Delight in the Things Your Child Creates

Expect your child to be creative. Applaud your child's creative efforts. Encourage your child to explore his or her creativity.

The child who feels appreciated for finding a new way to do, express, make, or view something is a child who feels confident in exploring the unknown. He or she is a child willing to take creative risks and who thus feels greater self-esteem. Such a child believes, "Mom and Dad like what I am able to create."

Many parents assume that creativity is only evident in certain children—that it's a talent or skill. Creativity is more like intelligence, every child has a dose of it! Just look at the use of language. Your child is going to come up with millions of brand new, never-before-spoken sentences during the course of growing up. No other person will ever string words together in the exact way that your child does. That's creativity!

Look at the way your child makes choices about clothes. That's your child's "style" under development. Nobody else will make those choices in exactly the same way. That's creativity!

Give your child a blank easel and fingerpaint, and

you'll see your child create a pattern that no other child in the room creates. Give your child a pencil and ask him to draw a picture, and you'll discover a picture that no other child in history has created.

Encourage your toddler to make up a dance. Let him or her delight in the way the body can move. Invite your teen to redecorate his or her room. Let your child know that it's OK to make up songs.

When faced with a choice between giving your young child a coloring book or a blank pad of paper, go for the blank pad because it requires more creativity.

When faced with the choice between taking your teenage daughter to the store for designer clothing, or giving your child sewing lessons and encouraging her to put together her own "look," opt for the sewing lessons.

You may set limits, of course, on the extent to which you will let your child experiment with his or her person or property. You have the parental prerogative of saying no to pink hair or crayon drawings on the wall of your living room. The point is to encourage creativity

- *that is within limits.*
  Your child will always face limits. Let him or her know that adulthood isn't a limit-free state. Express to your child, however, that true creativity flourishes within limits.
- *that turns chaos into beauty.*
  One mother says to her son, "I can hardly wait to see what a fine display of order you are going to

create out of this jungle presently known as Your Room."

- *that finds new uses for the ordinary.*
  Invite your child to make the centerpiece for your holiday table using anything found in the craft drawer or in the backyard.

From time to time, give items to your child and ask, "Can you think of anything else these could be used for before we throw them away?" One mother I know did that and found her daughter covering old laundry detergent boxes with contact paper to create containers for her magazines.

Give your child the freedom to try new spices on ordinary dishes. Try out new recipes with your child and new ways of presenting foods (in new containers, with unusual table decorations, in tins and on trays of the child's design).

The child who discovers his or her own creative abilities is a child who discovers his or her potential. And that is a child who values his or her uniqueness!

48 ■ The Value of a Pet

Give your child the opportunity of shouldering responsibility for another living creature—a puppy, a kitten, a hamster, or an animal of your choice!

Your child will learn several valuable lessons in caring for a pet.

He or she will learn that caring for another living creature is a daily responsibility. Animals need to be fed daily. They need fresh water daily. Point out to your child the many ways in which you take care of him or her, as your child, daily. One of the most important lifetime lessons that your child can learn is that childraising is a daily responsibility and a daily activity.

By caring for a pet your child will learn that all living creatures change as they grow. Puppies do not have the same needs, energy levels, or abilities as a full-grown dog. Draw parallels to your own child's development. Children need to be aware that people change and that life's changes are not only inevitable, but in most cases can be accommodated, whether it's change for the better or change for the worse.

By caring for a pet your child will learn that living creatures are born, grow to maturity, and die. The death of your child's pet is an important occasion. It's a time for serious discussion, and a time when you need to allow your child to feel sorrow. Don't dismiss the death of a pet as unimportant. Allow your child to grieve.

Death is an important fact of life for a child to learn about, a fact we often try to keep from a child. A very young child, of course, needs to be told about death in terms he or she can understand. Young children do, however, have a tremendous capacity to understand the concept of heaven and to imagine loved ones as having a life in a faraway place. Children find comfort in knowing that a loved one will never experience pain or sadness again.

Encourage involvement with a pet that your child can hold, talk to, and receive some kind of feedback from. I never recommend fish or a turtle as a pet. Look for a pet that has some "play" value with your child, an animal that your child can train or with which your child will enjoy spending time.

Some animals should not be pets. Easter bunnies and little ducks rarely make good pets. As cute and as desirable as they may seem in the early spring, these are animals that require special food, housing, and care that most people aren't prepared to give. Be aware that animals need space and sunshine. Apartments aren't good homes for many pets.

What if you live in a building that doesn't allow pets or a member of your family is allergic to pets? You can still provide your child an opportunity to be around animals. Take your child to the zoo. Visit petting zoos, too, where your child will have an opportunity to touch animals and to meet, face-to-face, animals he or she would never have as a pet. Visit a farm and observe farm animals with your child. You can also have a fun time with your child at county and state fairs as you explore the animal barns.

Being around animals with your child also provides you an opportunity to discuss issues such as the care of the environment (especially as it relates to endangered species), the uniqueness and diversity of creation, and the fact that animals come as male and female.

Association with animals provides your child an insight into his or her role as a caretaker for creation and the fact a child is one living creature among many.

Responsibility for a pet helps prepare your child for the responsibility of caring for others—perhaps even *you* in your old age!

A child who cares for animals knows, "Mom and Dad value me enough to leave me in charge or to let me help take care of another living creature. They trust me to promote life and know that I'm valuable to the life of my pet." A child who sees him or herself on the side of *life* has greater regard for his or her own life, as well as the lives of others.

49 ■ Apologize to Your Child When an Apology Is Due

When you know you've disappointed, hurt, or failed your child in some way admit it to your child. Apologize. Let your child know that you are sorry for what you have done and ask for forgiveness.

Your child will learn that apologies are not a sign of weakness but a sign of strength. Your child will grow in the confidence that he or she can apologize without losing respect or self-esteem.

Sometimes children express their hurt feelings as anger or silent pouting. When these behaviors are not directly related to a punishment (for example, the anger a child may feel at being sent to his room or grounded for hitting his little brother), ask your child why he or she is angry or giving you the silent treatment. Let your child know that you can take an honest response. Ask, "Did I disappoint you by something I did?" Or, "Did I let you down in some way?" Or, "Did I fail to come through for you when you needed me?" Or,

"Is there something you'd like me to do for you that I'm not doing?"

When your child says, "I wish you would . . ." or "I wish you wouldn't . . ." take time to listen. "I wish you wouldn't say that in front of my boyfriend, Mom!" "I wish you would have been on time so I wouldn't have had to put up with those kids who always tease me after school." "I wish you'd quit drinking so much."

Your child may "wish" for something you neither can do nor want to do. But, hear your child out. Take his or her expressed need into consideration. In some cases, you may need to ask for your child's help. In other cases, you may need to say, "What you are asking me to do is very difficult for me. I'll try. I may not be able to make this change. I don't want to disappoint you or hurt you, but I may not always be able to meet your expectations."

Ask your child to forgive you only if you are truly repentant. Don't be casual when you say, "Please forgive me." That will only cheapen your child's understanding of forgiveness.

Sometimes your child will take you by surprise in citing your weaknesses, faults, or errors. Rather than concede quickly or gush an apology, you may want to take time to consider your child's complaint. Be sure to let your child know your decision, however.

Apologize if an apology is due. Don't deal in self-justification, back peddle, or enter into a debate with your child. Apologize if you feel you need to; don't apologize if your child is wrong. Give and compromise where and when you can; don't be manipulated into concessions that are against your basic principles.

At times, you may need to let your child know that you have no intent of changing your behavior or original decision. "I'm sorry you're upset that I won't let you go to horror movies. I'm not going to change that rule." Give your child reasons why you must stand strong on some decisions. Give your child a few minutes to cool off or think things through.

A child who hears you apologize when you err is a child who can also apologize. He or she will learn how to move on in a relationship after an apology is given or received. A child who sees you stand firm in a decision will be a child who knows where he or she stands. He or she will learn that manipulation doesn't work and anger rarely has positive results.

A child with self-esteem is a child who knows that an apology won't depreciate personal value and that standing up for convictions is a mark of personal strength.

50 ■ Spontaneous Surprises and Unexpected Acts of Affection

Become a giver of spontaneous hugs, gifts, and words of praise. Let your child know, "Boy, I like you so much I just can't help telling you so!" Such a child feels truly appreciated, truly valued. And such a child grows in self-esteem.

Don't wait for special occasions. Don't even wait for your child to do something right.

Don't hold back the *joy* you feel at having your son or daughter as a member of your family!

"What's that for?" or "Where did that come from?" is likely to be your child's response to a giant bear hug or an unexpected present.

That's one time you can respond.

"Just because I like you."

"Just because I'm glad you're my child."

"Just because I'm thrilled that God created you."

"Just because the world seemed particularly bright today and one of the reasons is because you're in it!"

Put a note in your child's lunchbox to show you are

thinking about him or her and that you are hoping he or she is having a good day at school.

Put a flower in your child's room along with a note to let him or her know you think he or she is wonderful!

Mom, let your child know that you're grateful that you gave birth to him or her. Let your child know that he or she is the best gift you've ever received from God.

Let your son know you're glad he's a boy; let your daughter know you're glad she's a girl. Let your children know you are happy to be in their presence.

Let your child know that his or her life brings you fulfillment, joy, wonderment, and that he or she certainly always keeps your life "interesting."

Grin as you say it. Your child will know that you are really saying, "I wouldn't trade you for the world."

A child who is surprised by loving acts is a child who has self-esteem bolstered and reinforced in the most lasting, beneficial ways. Such a child comes to believe, "I seem to be valued all the time! I must be valuable!" Now that's self-esteem!

51 ■ Tell Your Child "I Love You"— and Do It with a Hug

Don't assume your child knows that you love him or her. Don't assume that all of your other phrases and compliments and words of approval are suitable substitutes for saying those three critically important words: "I love you."

Mean it when you say it and say it often. Assure your child that you loved him or her today, yesterday, and will love him or her tomorrow and forever.

"Do you know how much I love you? Do you really know?" Say it with warmth and your child will likely say, "Yeah, I *know.*"

I recently asked a child, "Do you know how much I love you?" She stared at me with a grin, "Of course I do. You tell me all the time."

"But do you really know it?"

"Sure!" she said. "Just put it on a test and ask me!"

Have you ever played the "How much do I love you?" game with your child? "How much do I love you? I love you as much as all the stars in the sky." Or, "I love you as much as all the fish in the sea."

My favorite response was that given by a five-year-old to her grandmother, "I love you as much as all the cat hairs on all the cats in the entire world."

Your child will never grow too old to hear you say, "I love you." It will mean as much to your child at age eighteen as it does at eight.

Your child is never too young to hear you say, "I love you." Tell it to your baby in the crib.

Whisper it into your child's ear as he or she sleeps. Tell it to your child as you change diapers or give a bath. Write it in a card that you send to your child at camp.

Let your child know you love him or her for the very fact that he or she *exists.*

Let your child know that your love cannot be destroyed.

Let your child know that your love is a divine gift. "My love for you is just something God gave me in a big dose. I don't know why or how He did it. I just know He did, and there's not a thing I can do about it. You're just stuck with the fact that I love you!"

Love is the foundation on which self-esteem is built. If children don't know they are loved they will have an extremely difficult time believing they have value. Children may feel a parent's respect and approval, but that will never make up for a giant dose of unadultered, unprovoked, unlimited love!

Your love is the foundation for your child's self-esteem and confidence. Don't withhold the good news of your love from your child!